# bridge conventions

## A Guide to Understanding Techniques of Modern Bidding

Edwin B. Kantar

*Melvin Powers*
*Wilshire Book Company*

12015 Sherman Road, No. Hollywood, CA 91605

Library of Congress Catalog Number: 73-187974

ISBN-0-87980-013-5

Printed in the United States of America

# I N D E X

# INTRODUCTION

What I have tried to do in this book is clarify some of the more popular conventions. I have noticed that many bridge players use a convention after hearing a one or two sentence explanation and then think they can handle it. Hah! Although I have no proof I would be willing to bet that more disasters than successes come from the use of a new convention until both partners understand it rather well.

Intervening bids in particular have an annoying way of fouling up a convention unless there has been prior discussion. Also, responding to an artificial or conventional bid can be troublesome.

In any case I have tried to go further than most books in explaining the more popular conventions such as Stayman, Jacoby, Blackwood, Negative Doubles, Limit Raises, etc. Now if you really wish to play these conventions you will have more than the basics at your disposal.

My final bit of advice is to only use conventions that you and your partner understand and to try to get by with as few as possible until you have mastered the ones you play. Then, perhaps you can add one at a time until you know so many and are so thoroughly confused (join the club) that you will wish that you had never even heard of the word.

EDWIN B. KANTAR

## THE STAYMAN CONVENTION

Next to "Blackwood" and the takeout double, "Stayman" is the most widely used bridge convention in the world.

Basically, it is a simple convention--a response of either 2C to 1NT or 3C to 2NT is used to cover a 4-4 or a 5-3 major suit fit; however, extensions and modifications have caused confusion.

In my opinion, Stayman should be used in conjunction with the Jacoby Transfer when responding to either one or two no trump. Most experts share this belief. However, for those who do not use the Jacoby Transfer, "Forcing Stayman" is best. Forcing Stayman means that the 2C response is forcing to 2NT or three of a major.

### When to Use Stayman in Response to 1NT

Basically, the convention should be used any time responder has one or two four card majors and at least 8 H.C.P.

Assume partner opens 1NT and you hold:

| | (1) | (2) |
|---|---|---|
| | S. AJ87 | S. KQ98 |
| | H. K765 | H. 54 |
| | D. 54 | D. AJ76 |
| | C. 765 | C. 654 |

With either of these hands, respond 2C to ask opener if he has a four card major. If opener has a four card major, he bids it; if not, he rebids 2D. If opener rebids 2D, responder knows there is no eight card major suit fit and rebids 2NT with (1) and 3NT with (2), the same number of no trump he would have bid had he not used Stayman.

Simple, isn't it? A few things to watch out for when using Stayman are:

(1) Do not use Stayman with a 4-3-3-3 hand. Simply raise N.T.

(2) Do not use Stayman if the doubleton is very strong, the major is very weak, and the hand counts to 11-14-H.C.P. Hands like this often play better in no trump and avoid the risk of bad trump breaks.

Examples of hands that do not use Stayman in response to 1NT:

| (1) | (2) | (3) |
|---|---|---|
| S. A765 | S. K543 | S. 8765 |
| H. K76 | H. 1098 | H. AQ |
| D. Q87 | D. AJ6 | D. KQ98 |
| C. J87 | C. 976 | C. 876 |

With (1) respond 3NT to show 10-14- H.C.P. 4-3-3-3 distribution.

With (2) respond 2NT to show 8-9- H.C.P. 4-3-3-3 distribution.

With (3) respond 3NT. Strong doubleton 11-14- H.C.P.

## The Unusual Hand that Uses Stayman

There is one type of hand that uses Stayman without the required 8 H.C.P. It is a hand that has a singleton or void in CLUBS, three four-card suits, or one five-card suit and two four-card suits.

```
(1)   S. 8765        (2)   S. J987        (3)   S. Q876
      H. A876              H. 76543             H. J765
      D. 107654            D. Q876              D. 10987
      C. Void              C. Void              C. 2
```

Any of these hands may safely use Stayman as any rebid opener makes will be passed, including 2D.

## Responding Hands With Five Card Majors

Stayman is not used with five card major suits when the Jacoby Transfer Bid is being used. When not playing Jacoby, Stayman is used with five card majors. A minimum of 7 H.C.P. is required.

Partner opens 1NT and you hold:

```
(1)   S. AQ765       (2)   S. K876        (3)   S. 6
      H. K76               H. AQ987             H. A9876
      D. 54                D. J4                D. 54
      C. 765               C. 54                C. KQ876
```

Each of these hands responds 2C to an opening bid of 1NT and shows the major on the rebid. WHEN THE STAYMAN BIDDER FOLLOWS UP HIS 2C RESPONSE WITH THE BID OF A MAJOR, HE IS DESCRIBING A FIVE CARD SUIT. WITH A FOUR CARD MAJOR, THE RESPONDER MUST EITHER RETURN TO NO TRUMP OR RAISE OPENER'S MAJOR. THE 2C BIDDER MAY NEVER NAME A FOUR CARD MAJOR.

| Opener | (1) Responder | (2) Responder |
|---|---|---|
| S. AJ8 | S. K10754 | S. K1076 |
| H. K87 | H. A2 | H. A2 |
| D. AQ76 | D. J1043 | D. J1043 |
| C. K87 | C. 96 | C. 943 |

```
(1)   1NT    2C       (2)   1NT    2C
      2D     2S             2D     2NT
      3S     4S             3NT    Pass
```

In (1) responder employs Stayman with a five card major and then bids the major to show a five card suit and at least 8 points (seven H.C.P. and a five card suit). 2S is a one round force. Opener raises to 3S or 4S with three card support and rebids 2NT or 3NT with a doubleton spade. (Playing non-forcing Stayman responder's 2S rebid can be passed).

In (2), responder uses Stayman with a four card major. Once responder sees no 4-4 major fit exists, he immediately retreats to no trump, showing his point count en route.

When responder holds less than 8 points with a five card major, he either passes or bids two of the major directly which is a sign-off. If responder bids 2C and then the major, he is interested in game.

```
(1)   S. AJ987        (2)   S. Q9765
      H. 2                  H. Q54
      D. 5432              D. J4
      C. 543               C. 765
```

With (1), respond 2S to 1NT showing less than 8 points. With (2), either pass (best) or respond 2S. 5-3-3-2 hands often play better in no trump, particularly if partner has a small doubleton in your five card suit and a good five card suit of his own.

## Six Card Majors

In general, Stayman is not used with a six card major suit. Responder bids the suit directly at the two, three or four level, depending upon strength.

1NT-2H  Could show either a five or six card suit. It is a signoff,
1NT-2S  so holding a six card suit responder will have, at most, 5-6 H.C.P.

1NT-3H  This promises a good six card suit with some slam aspirations.
1NT-3S  The normal range for this bid is 13-15 points. If responder has more, he takes charge later.

1NT-4H  These responses also promise six card suits, but no slam
1NT-4S  aspirations. They describe a hand that has 8-12 points.

```
(1)   S. QJ9876       (2)   S. AQJ876      (3)   S. KJ10765
      H. 2                  H. K43               H. 2
      D. 765               D. Q2                D. Q876
      C. 654               C. 87                C. J4
```

(1)  Respond 2S. Partner passes unless he has 18 points, in which case, he raises to 3S.

(2)  Respond 3S. Tell partner you have some slam interest. If partner is interested in a slam, he will cue bid four of some suit. If he is minimum, he will rebid 3NT or 4S.

(3)  Respond 4S. Because you think you can make it.

One possible use of Stayman with a six card major is this otherwise wasted sequence when playing Forcing Stayman:

| Opener | Responder | Opener | Responder |
|--------|-----------|--------|-----------|
| 1NT | 2C | 1NT | 2C |
| 2D | 3H or 3S | 2S | 4H |

What does this mean?  It could mean that responder is making a slam try with a WEAK SIX CARD MAJOR.  This contrasts to the immediate jump which shows a slam try with a strong six card major.

| Opener | Responder |
|--------|-----------|
| 1NT | 3H or 3S |

For example:   
S. Q108765   If partner opens 1NT, respond 2C
H. A4   and then jump in spades to show
D. KJ7   a weak six card suit interested
C. K3   in slam.

## The Minor Suits

Those homeless orphans, the minor suits.  Hands that have five or six card minor suits, and no singletons or voids, usually play best in no trump.

(1)  S. A6      (2)  S. K5
      H. 876           H. 654
      D. KQ876      D. AJ10876
      C. 765           C. 54

Both of these hands are automatic responses of 3NT to an opening bid of 1NT.  Responder adds one point for a usable five card suit and two points for a usable six card suit when responding to 1NT.

The problem hands are the unbalanced minor suit hands.  They might be:

      (1)  Sign-off hands.
      (2)  Invitational game hands.
      (3)  Game hands.
      (4)  Invitational slam hands.

It has always been difficult to construct a method for handling all of these types without imposing a tremendous amount of memory strain on the reader.  Therefore, I am going to suggest that you play a method that does not cater to (1) but will help you handle the others.

## A.  With Weak Six Card Minor Suits

(1)  S. 5      (2)  S. 5
      H. J76          H. J76
      D. QJ10765    D. 876
      C. 543         C. QJ10765

If partner opens 1NT, respond 2D with (1), a sign-off.  However, with (2), simply pass!  If the opponents double, bid 2C.  (Not Stayman after a double.)  YOU SIMPLY CAN'T SIGN OFF IN CLUBS!

4

## B. With Invitational Six Card Minor Suits

Remember we are opening 1NT with small doubletons. This means that when responder is looking at KQxxxx and no side entry he can no longer be sure that the suit will run at no trump. Therefore respond 3C or 3D with 6-7 H.C.P. and a six card suit to invite 3NT IF PARTNER HAS A FIT. With a small doubleton in the minor or a minimum no trump opener passes.

| | (1) | S. 54 | (2) | S. 653 |
|---|---|---|---|---|
| | | H. QJ4 | | H. 876 |
| | | D. KJ10876 | | D. 2 |
| | | C. 54 | | C. AQ10765 |

With (1) respond 3D and with (2) respond 3C. Partner can pass either of these responses.

## C. With Game Going or Slammish Hands
## With Six Card Minor Suits

These hands bid 2C first and then the minor. This is forcing to game.

| | (1) | S. K8 | (2) | S. KQ76 |
|---|---|---|---|---|
| | | H. A4 | | H. 4 |
| | | D. 876 | | D. AJ10765 |
| | | C. AQ7654 | | C. 43 |

Hand (1) responds 2C and then 3C to show an interest in a club game or slam. Hand (2) responds 2C (maybe there is a spade fit) and then 3D to show a strong hand in diamonds.

This may not be the best way to handle the minor suits but it is the easiest. All you give up is your signoff in clubs.

## Tips to the No Trump Opener After Partner Has Responded 2C

1. With no four card major, rebid 2D unless you have opened 1NT with a broken six card minor (this is possible). In that case rebid your minor at the three level.

| Opener | Responder | |
|---|---|---|
| 1NT | 2C | |
| 3C or 3D | | (shows a broken six card minor) |

If your six card minor is solid, rebid 2NT.

| Opener | Responder |
|---|---|
| 1NT | 2C |
| 2NT | |

2. If you have opened 1NT with a five card major, rebid three of your major, not two.

| Opener | Responder | |
|---|---|---|
| 1NT | 2C | |
| 3H or 3S | | (shows a five card major) |

3. If you have two four card majors, bid your better major. If partner then retreats to no trump bid the other major. He must have one four card major if he responds 2C and then rebids no trump.

4. Respect partner's signoffs. Responses of 2D, 2H or 2S mean partner is not interested in game. Pass unless you have 18 points plus a fit. In that case give a single raise.

## Tips to the Stayman Bidder

1. Do not use Stayman unless you have at least 7 H.C.P. with a five card major or 8 H.C.P. with a four card major.

2. Do not use Stayman with a 4-3-3-3 hand.

3. Do not use Styaman with a six card major suit. (One exception noted earlier.)

4. Discuss with your partner whether you are playing Forcing or Non-Forcing Stayman. The difference revolves around this sequence:

| Opener | Responder |
|--------|-----------|
| 1NT    | 2C        |
| 2D     | 2S        |

Playing Forcing Stayman, the 2S rebid is a one round force. Playing Non-Forcing Stayman, it can be passed if opener is minimum. Therefore playing Non-Forcing Stayman responder is obliged to jump to three of his five card major on his rebid with ten or more points.

A direct jump to three of a major describes a six card suit and 13-15 points.

# Examples of Forcing Stayman

| Opener | Responder | Opener | Responder | |
|---|---|---|---|---|
| S. AJ4 | S. 10965 | 1NT | 2C | Responder shows 8-9. |
| H. K76 | H. A1083 | 2D | 2NT | |
| D. Q43 | D. A9 | Pass | | |
| C. AQ54 | C. 976 | | | |
| S. K5 | S. A10762 | 1NT | 2C | (Responder shows a five card spade suit, 8 or more points.) Opener shows a doubleton spade and a minimum no trump. |
| H. AJ75 | H. 32 | 2H | 2S | |
| D. K875 | D. Q95 | 2NT | 3NT | |
| C. AJ3 | C. K95 | Pass | | |
| S. AK765 | S. Q103 | 1NT | 2C | Opener shows a five card spade suit. |
| H. K2 | H. A987 | 3S | 4S | |
| D. AJ7 | D. 32 | Pass | | |
| C. J98 | C. Q1076 | | | |
| S. AJ | S. K654 | 1NT | 2C | Opener shows a broken six card diamond suit. Responder knows the hand is a misfit. With a slightly stronger hand, responder rebids 3NT. |
| H. K98 | H. QJ43 | 3D | Pass | |
| D. QJ9854 | D. 2 | | | |
| C. A10 | C. Q765 | | | |
| S. AQ5 | S. KJ43 | 1NT | 2C | Responder makes a mild slam try in diamonds. Opener accepts and cues his spade strength. Responder shows his spade honor. Opener cue bids the ace of clubs. Responder bids the slam with the singleton heart. |
| H. Q76 | H. 2 | 2D | 3D | |
| D. KJ76 | D. AQ9876 | 3S | 4S | |
| C. AQ6 | C. K4 | 5C | 6D | |
| | | Pass | | |
| S. K876 | S. QJ53 | 1NT | 2C | Responder uses Stayman with only 7 H.C.P. which is acceptable with both majors and a side singleton. Responder raises, but opener refuses the invitation with a minimum. |
| H. A76 | H. J854 | 2S | 3S | |
| D. QJ7 | D. K654 | Pass | | |
| C. KQJ | C. 2 | | | |
| S. KQ7 | S. 1098 | 1NT | 2H | Opener must pass unless he holds 18 H.C.P. in which case he should raise to 3H or (by agreement) bid 2NT to show two of the top three honors in responder's suit so responder can gamble on a no trump game. |
| H. A87 | H. J106532 | Pass | | |
| D. KQ5 | D. 94 | | | |
| C. Q876 | C. K4 | | | |
| S. AQ4 | S. K107532 | 1NT | 2S | Responder signs off but opener rebids 2NT to show a maximum and two of the top three spade honors. Responder gambles 3NT knowing there must be six fast spade tricks. |
| H. K75 | H. J5 | 2NT | 3NT | |
| D. AQ4 | D. J8 | Pass | | |
| C. K632 | C. 1054 | | | |

7

## Two-Way Stayman

Two-Way Stayman is another variation of the Stayman Convention. Using this method, responses of 2C and 2D to a 1NT opening are both Stayman. A response of 2C asks for a major, but warns partner the hand is not in the game zone. Responder is simply searching for a part score unless opener happens to have a super fit plus a maximum.

However, an original response of 2D is also Stayman but forcing to game.

This is a reasonable variation of Stayman, but it has drawbacks:

(1) You can no longer bid 2D naturally.

(2) The opponents know the strength of responder's hand and are more apt to compete after a 2C response.

(3) The opponents can double either 2C or 2D for a lead.

(4) You cannot use Jacoby Transfer responses.

# RESPONSES TO 1NT (16-18) USING FORCING STAYMAN

| Opener | Responder | Meaning |
|--------|-----------|---------|
| 1NT | 2C | Stayman. |
| 1NT | *2C/minimum bid in major | Five card suit. Forcing. |
| 1NT | 2C/jump in major | Weak six card suit. Slam try. |
| 1NT | 2C/3C or 3D | Forcing to game. |
| 1NT | 2C/2NT | 8-9 balanced. (Must have at least one four card major.) |
| 1NT | 2C/3NT | 10-14 balanced. (Must have at least one four card major.) |
| 1NT | 2C/4NT | 15-16 balanced. (Must have at least one four card major.) |
| 1NT | 2C/4C | Gerber. |
| 1NT | 2D, 2H, 2S | Sign-offs. |
| 1NT | 2NT | 8-9 balanced. |
| 1NT | 3C, 3D | Invitational to game. |
| 1NT | 3H, 3S | Good six card major. Slam try. |
| 1NT | 3NT | 10-14 balanced. |
| 1NT | 4C | Gerber. |
| 1NT | 4D | Seldom used. |
| 1NT | 4H, 4S | Sign-offs. |
| 1NT | 4NT | 15-16 balanced. |

* This mark "/" means followed by. In other words a response of 2C followed by a minimum rebid in a major suit shows five cards in that suit and is forcing.

| Opener | Responder | Meaning |
|---|---|---|
| 2NT | 3C | Stayman. |
| 2NT | 3C/3H or 3S | Five card suit. Forcing. |
| 2NT | 3C/3NT | 5-10. Must have at least one four card major. |
| 2NT | 3C/4H or 4S | Slam try. Six card suit. |
| 2NT | 3C/4C | Gerber. |
| 2NT | 3C/4D | Slam try in diamonds, probably a four card major suit on the side. |
| 2NT | 3D, 3H, 3S | Forcing to game. Five or six card suits. |
| 2NT | 3NT | 5-10 balanced. |
| 2NT | *4C | Gerber. |
| 2NT | 4D | Slam try in diamonds. |
| 2NT | 4H, 4S | Sign-offs. |
| 2NT | 4NT | 11-12 balanced. |

* It is possible to use this sequence as a slam try in clubs and only use Gerber when four clubs is preceded by three clubs.

The Jacoby Transfer Bid (JTB) is based on the bridge truism that a hand will generally play better in either suit or no trump if the stronger of the two hands is the declarer. As this convention is used after opening bids of one or two no trump, the idea is to force the no trump opener to play the hand in responder's long suit if necessary!

Responder does this by simply bidding the suit BENEATH his long major suit which forces the opening no trump bidder to bid responder's real suit. This is known as completing the transfer.

| Opener | Responder |
|--------|-----------|
| 1NT | 2D |
| 2H | ? |

| Opener | Responder |
|--------|-----------|
| 1NT | 2H |
| 2S | ? |

| Opener | Responder |
|--------|-----------|
| 2NT | 3D |
| 3H | ? |

| Opener | Responder |
|--------|-----------|
| 2NT | 3H |
| 3S | ? |

These are the four most common beginnings of JTB sequences. The responder now has many options at his disposal, but if the hand does play in responder's major, the opener will always be the declarer forcing the defenders to lead up to the stronger hand.

### When to Use the JTB

Normally, the responder will use the JTB any time he holds a five or six card major suit (or seven or eight for that matter), with two noteworthy exceptions:

1. With a terrible hand and a five card major suit (three high card points or less) and a distribution of 5-3-3-2, in the long run it is better to pass the opening one no trump bid. But with 5-4-2-2 or 5-4-3-1 and a weak hand transfer into the five card major and then pass.

2. With five or six cards in one major suit and four cards in the other and a minimum of 7 H.C.P. Stayman is used rather than Jacoby.

In all other cases, Jacoby is used after partner opens one no trump and responder has a five or six card major suit.

## With a Five Card Major Suit

Responder must remember that when he makes a transfer bid, he promises five cards in his suit. Therefore, if responder then raises the opener who has been compelled to mention the responder's suit, the responder is showing a six card suit.

The most common sequences are:

| Opener | Responder |  | Opener | Responder |
|--------|-----------|--|--------|-----------|
| S. A1075 | S. 2 |  | 1NT | 2D |
| H. K42 | H. 109753 |  | 2H | Pass |
| D. AQ8 | D. J42 |  |  |  |
| C. K65 | C. A874 |  |  |  |

Responder can have either a five or six card heart suit, but he obviously has a very weak hand that offers no promise for game.

| Opener | Responder |  | Opener | Responder |
|--------|-----------|--|--------|-----------|
| S. AQx | S. Kx |  | 1NT | 2D |
| H. Kx | H. J9xxx |  | 2H | 2NT |
| D. Qxxx | D. Axx |  | Pass |  |
| C. AJxx | C. xxx |  |  |  |

Responder shows five hearts and the strength of a raise to two no trump. Opener with a minimum and only a doubleton heart passes.

| Opener | Responder |  | Opener | Responder |
|--------|-----------|--|--------|-----------|
| S. Axx | S. KJ10xx |  | 1NT | 2H |
| H. QJ | H. xxx |  | 2S | 2NT |
| D. Axxx | D. Kx |  | 3S | Pass |
| C. KQxx | C. xxx |  |  |  |

Again responder shows a hand in the 7-9 H.C.P. range with a five card spade suit. This time opener elects to play the hand in the known 5-3 fit because of his probable heart weakness and also because he has probable ruffing value with his doubleton heart. Responder passes because opener could have leaped to four spades over two no trump if he liked his hand a little better.

| Opener | Responder |  | Opener | Responder |
|--------|-----------|--|--------|-----------|
| S. Kx | S. Qxxxx |  | 1NT | 2H |
| H. K98x | H. x |  | 2S | 3D |
| D. Q9x | D. AJ10xx |  | 3NT | Pass |
| C. AKJx | C. Qx |  |  |  |

Responder has shown five spades by his two heart bid so he never need rebid the suit. His three diamond rebid shows a two suiter (usually 5-5) and is forcing to game. Opener with good stoppers in the unbid suits elects to play the hand in no trump. Had opener three spades, he would probably elect to play in spades, the known 5-3 fit.

This brings us to a touchy problem. If a transfer followed by a new suit shows 5-5 and is forcing to game, what do we do with weaker 5-5 hands?

| Opener | Responder |  | Opener | Responder |
|--------|-----------|--|--------|-----------|
| S. K10 | S. Jxxxx  |  | 1NT | 2H |
| H. AQxx | H. x     |  | 2S | Pass |
| D. xxxx | D. xx    |  | | |
| C. AQJ | C. Kxxxx  |  | | |

This may not be as good a contract as a partial in clubs, but it is the best we can do given the system we are playing. Many times opener will have three or even four spades and a game can be reached. (Remember, opener jumps to 3S over 2H to show a super maximum.)

| Opener | Responder |  | Opener | Responder |
|--------|-----------|--|--------|-----------|
| S. Kxx | S. AJxxx  |  | 1NT | 2H |
| H. Axx | H. x      |  | 2S | 3S |
| D. KQxx | D. xx    |  | 4S | Pass |
| C. AJx | C. Qxxxx  |  | | |

This is the ONLY time responder can transfer and raise immediately with a five card suit. He must have a two suiter that is not strong enough to force to game by bidding the second suit. (Usually 6-8 high card points). Opener will assume responder has six spades on this auction but that is life.

*NOTE: With specifically five hearts and five spades and a game going hand, responder should use Stayman. With an invitational hand, Jacoby. The sequence:

| Opener | Responder |
|--------|-----------|
| 1NT | 2H |
| 2S | 3H |
| ? | |

shows a 5-5 major hand...is not forcing.

| Opener | Responder | | Opener | Responder |
|--------|-----------|---|--------|-----------|
| S. Kx | S. AQxxx | | 1NT | 2H |
| H. Axxx | H. Qx | | 2S | 3NT |
| D. J10xx | D. Qxx | | Pass | |
| C. AKJ | C. xxx | | | |

In this sequence, one of the most common, responder shows five spades, a balanced hand pattern (either 5-3-3-2 or 5-4-2-2) and 9-13 high card points.

Opener bids as follows:

1. With a doubleton spade he automatically passes.

2. With three spades and an unstopped suit or a doubleton, he bids four spades.

3. With three spades and 4-3-3-3 distribution and no unstopped suit, he passes.

4. With four spades, he bids four spades.

| Opener | Responder | | Opener | Responder |
|--------|-----------|---|--------|-----------|
| S. Ax | S. KQx | | 1NT | 2D |
| H. Kxx | H. AQJxx | | 2H | 4NT |
| D. AQxxx | D. Kxx | | 6H | Pass |
| C. KJx | C. xx | | | |

Responder shows five hearts and the strength to raise to 4NT (14-15 high card points). Opener accepts by bidding six hearts because he has a good hand for hearts. With a doubleton heart he would either pass with a minimum or jump to six no trump with a maximum. This is not Blackwood.

## Asking for Aces Using the JTB

If the responding bidder wishes to ask for aces, he can either jump to 4C immediately (Gerber) or he can transfer at the four level (Texas) and then bid 4NT which is Blackwood.

| Opener | Responder | | Opener | Responder |
|--------|-----------|---|--------|-----------|
| S. K10x | S. x | | 1NT | 4D |
| H. Kxx | H. AQJ10xx | | 4H | 4NT |
| D. AQJx | D. xx | | 5D | 6H |
| C. QJx | C. AK109 | | Pass | |

Responder transfers to 4H and then asks for aces by bidding four no trump. The hand now plays in 6H from the opener's side. Using the transfer at the four level has the dual effect of insuring that the hand is played from the strong side and clarifying the meaning of four no trump after a transfer. 4NT after a two level transfer is natural and can be passed, but after a four level transfer, it is Blackwood.

## The JTB With Six Card Major Suits

Although it is possible not to use the JTB with a five card major and a very weak balanced hand, Jacoby is almost always used with a six card major. Normally, the responding hand will either want to play the hand in a part score, invite game, or play in game. This is how he goes about it with a six card major and no slam aspirations.

| Opener | Responder | Opener | Responder |
|---|---|---|---|
| S. AQxx | S. xx | 1NT | 2D |
| H. Jx | H. K10xxxx | 2H | Pass |
| D. Kxxx | D. Jx | | |
| C. AQx | C. xxx | | |

Responder with 5 H.C.P. or less, transfers and then passes as game is very remote.

| Opener | Responder | Opener | Responder |
|---|---|---|---|
| S. KQxx | S. Axx | 1NT | 2D |
| H. 10x | H. K9xxxx | 2H | 3H |
| D. AQxx | D. xx | Pass | |
| C. AJx | C. xx | | |

In this sequence, responder promises a six card suit and 6-7 H.C.P. Opener with a minimum passes.

| Opener | Responder | Opener | Responder |
|---|---|---|---|
| S. Kxx | S. x | 1NT | 4D |
| H. Qx | H. AJ10xxx | 4H | Pass |
| D. AJxxx | D. Qx | | |
| C. KQJ | C. 10xxx | | |

Responder wishes to be in game but no higher. Although he has only 7 H.C.P. he has good distribution. He transfers to the four level and then passes. In order to bid this way and have little or no chance to miss a slam, the responder might have as little as 7 H.C.P. with good distribution on up to 11 H.C.P. with poor

distribution (6-3-2-2). If responder is stronger he either
jumps to three of his major immediately which is a strong slam
try, 14-15 H.C.P., or transfers at the two level and then raises
to game, 11-13 H.C.P., a milder slam try. This raise to game
after a two level transfer can only be used in conjunction with
four level transfers. Otherwise, it is a sign-off.

## Refusing a Transfer

Ninety-five times out of a hundred, when the responder makes a transfer
bid at the two level the opener will complete the transfer at the two
level. However, the opener has other options. He can refuse the transfer by bidding two no trump. This shows a small doubleton in the transfer suit and _double_ or _triple_ stoppers in the other suits.

| Opener | Responder | | Opener | Responder |
|--------|-----------|--|--------|-----------|
| S. xx | S. Kxxxx | | 1NT | 2H |
| H. AQ10x | H. xx | | 2NT | Pass |
| D. KQ9x | D. Jxxx | | | |
| C. AQ10 | C. xx | | | |

Opener refuses to complete the transfer and instead rebids 2NT,
a rarity. Responder passes. If the responder wishes to insist
upon his suit, he once again bids the suit beneath his real suit
and this time the opener must comply.

| Opener | Responder | | Opener | Responder |
|--------|-----------|--|--------|-----------|
| S. xx | S. KJ9xxx | | 1NT | 2H |
| H. AQ10x | H. xx | | 2NT | 3H |
| D. KQ9x | D. x | | 3S | Pass |
| C. AQ10 | C. Jxxx | | | |

A far more common occurrence is for the opener to jump in the transfer
suit to show a super maximum for responder's suit.

| Opener | Responder | | Opener | Responder |
|--------|-----------|--|--------|-----------|
| S. Axxx | S. Qxxxx | | 1NT | 2H |
| H. Kx | H. xxx | | 3S | 4S |
| D. AQxx | D. Kxxx | | Pass | |
| C. A10x | C. x | | | |

Responder bids 2H intending to pass 2S. However, when opener
shows a super hand for spades by jumping to 3S, opener gambles
on 4S. Responder must always remember that opener cannot have
a super hand for his major suit if he does not jump.

16

## When a Transfer Bid Has Been Doubled

Just as the opponents will double an artificial Stayman bid of 2C for a club lead, so will they double responder's artificial responses of 2D and 2H.

Assume for the moment that the bidding has proceeded as follows:

| South | West | North | East |
|-------|------|-------|------|
| 1NT | Pass | 2H | Dbl. |
| ? | | | |

What should South do over the double?

   With a doubleton spade and less than four or five hearts he should pass.

   With a doubleton spade and four or five good hearts he should redouble.

   With three or four spades and a minimum hand he should bid 2S.

   With three or four spades and a maximum hand he should jump to 3S.

## After an Opening Bid of 2NT

JTB's are used identically after an opening bid of 2NT. Everything applies. Furthermore, JTB's are also used after a sequence that begins like this:

| Opener | Responder |
|--------|-----------|
| 2C* | 2D** |
| 2NT | ? |

   *Artificial and strong.

   **Negative response.

Responder now uses the JTB just as if the opener has opened two no trump. Remember, JTB can be used in conjunction with Stayman. Only now Stayman is used primarily for hands that have FOUR card majors or one five card major and one four card major.

In the above sequence, JTB's are used only if the original response to the 2C opening was 2D.

## JTB After Interference

All transfer sequences are off if the player directly following the opening 1NT bidder overcalls or doubles. Remember: NO JACOBY TRANSFER BIDS AFTER INTERFERENCE.

## JTB After a 1NT Overcall

| South | West | North | East |
|-------|------|-------|------|
| Pass | 1D | 1NT | Pass |
| ? | | | |

This is optional but if you really dig JTB's and understand them you can use them here too. Just assume your partner has opened 1NT and bid accordingly using Stayman (2C) and your transfer responses of 2D and 2H or 4D and 4H. As a matter of fact it is easier to play the same way after a 1NT opening or overcall. There is less to remember. But again, if there is interference to the right - NO JACOBY.

## The Two Spade Response

Until this time we have dealt entirely with responding hands that hold long major suits and have transferred the play to the opener's side. What about the minors?

The 2S response can be used to show various minor suited hands. There are currently many treatments for the 2S response. I will give you the one I like best.

The 2S response is made with any of the following types of hands:

1. Any minor two suiter (5-5 or 6-5).

2. Any hand that wishes to sign off in DIAMONDS.

3. Any hand that has either 5-4 or 4-4 in the minors with no singleton and 14-15 H.C.P.

## How Does Opener Rebid When Responder Bids 2S?

With no four card minor he rebids 2NT.

With a four or five card minor he bids it.

| Opener | Responder | | Opener | Responder |
|--------|-----------|--|--------|-----------|
| S. AJxx | S. x | | 1NT | 2S |
| H. K10xx | H. xx | | 2NT | 3C |
| D. Qxx | D. K10xxx | | 3D | Pass |
| C. AQ | C. J10xxx | | | |

18

Opener denies a four card minor and responder shows a WEAK MINOR
two suiter by rebidding 3C. Opener must either pass or bid 3D.
Had opener bid either 3C or 3D over 2S, responder would have passed.

| Opener | Responder | | Opener | Responder |
|--------|-----------|--|--------|-----------|
| S. Qxx | S. x | | 1NT | 2S |
| H. AKxx | H. xx | | 2NT | 3S |
| D. KJx | D. Axxxx | | 4C | 5C |
| C. Axx | C. KQxxx | | | |

Opener denies a four card minor and responder shows a GAME GOING
minor two suiter by bidding the SINGLETON. (If responder had a
weak minor two suiter, he would rebid 3C over 2NT). Opener warned
of the weakness in spades elects to play the hand in a minor suit.

If opener were stronger in spades, he might elect to play the hand
in three no trump regardless.

| Opener | Responder | | Opener | Responder |
|--------|-----------|--|--------|-----------|
| S. Q10xx | S. Kx | | 1NT | 2S |
| H. AKJx | H. x | | 2NT | 3H |
| D. Kx | D. QJxxx | | 3NT | Pass |
| C. Axx | C. KJ10xx | | | |

Responder shows a singleton heart with a game going minor two suiter. Opener judges to play 3NT with his major suit strength. Responder might also elect to bid this way with 5-4-3-1 hands - both
long suits being the minors, of course.

| Opener | Responder | | Opener | Responder |
|--------|-----------|--|--------|-----------|
| S. Kx | S. Qxxx | | 1NT | 2S |
| H. Kxxx | H. x | | 3C | 3D |
| D. AQx | D. J10xxxx | | Pass | |
| C. A10xx | C. xx | | | |

This is how responder signs off in diamonds. Opener must pass.
(If responder had a weak minor two suiter, he would pass 3C - if
he had a strong minor two suiter, he would show his singleton on
the rebid). Notice that responder does not use Stayman with such
a hand, as it is impossible to get untracked if opener does not
have four spades. You always get too high.

Using the above method, there is no way to sign off in clubs, un-

less you use this sequence as a sign-off:

| Opener | Responder |
|--------|-----------|
| 1NT | 2C |
| 2D,2H,2S | 3C |

Most experts, however, use the above sequence as forcing to describe a hand with a four card major and a five or six card club suit that is interested in game and perhaps slam.

It is not so serious not to be able to sign-off in clubs. With a club bust, simply pass. If either opponent doubles, you can then bid your club suit.

| Opener | Responder | | Opener | Responder |
|--------|-----------|---|--------|-----------|
| S. AJxx | S. Kx | | 1NT | 2S |
| H. K10x | H. AJx | | 2NT | 3NT |
| D. KJx | D. Q10xx | | Pass | |
| C. KJx | C. Axxx | | | |

Responder shows a balanced minor two suiter with no singleton and 14-15 high card points. Opener with only 16 H.C.P. elects to pass, but slam is very close. Had opener shown a four card minor, responder would probably carry the hand to slam himself.

If this all seems too much to bear, you might try doing as thousands have done before you...forget the whole thing. Or better, limit your transfer sequences to 2D and 2H over 1NT and 3D and 3H over 2NT. Even that ought to be enough to improve your accuracy in no trump bidding.

# TIPS ON JACOBY

1. A transfer bid promises a five card major. If responder later raises he shows a six card suit.

2. Jacoby cannot be used if the 1NT opening bid is either overcalled or doubled.

3. Jacoby is used at the two and four levels over a 1NT opening bid. Not at the three level.

4. After a 2NT opening bid, Jacoby is used at either the three or four level.

5. Responder cannot sign off at 2D when playing Jacoby.

6. Responder bids according to his distribution and point count. With 5-3-3-2 or 5-4-2-2, responder transfers and then rebids no trump. With 5-5-2-1, responder transfers and then bids his second suit if he has eight or more H.C.P. With less, responder transfers and either passes or raises.

7. With a six card major responder either transfers and passes, transfers and raises to three, transfers at the four level, transfers and raises to four, or jumps to three of his suit depending upon his strength.

8. A transfer at the two level followed by 4NT is natural, not Blackwood.

9. A transfer at the four level followed by 4NT is Blackwood.

10. If you play transfers at the four level and one player forgets the other one must have a good sense of humor.

11. If you are not playing with someone who has a good sense of humor - GOOD LUCK!

# CAPSULE SUMMARY
## RESPONSES TO 1NT USING FORCING STAYMAN AND JACOBY TRANSFER

| Opener | Responder | Meaning |
|--------|-----------|---------|
| 1NT | 2C | Stayman. |
| 1NT | 2C/2H or 2S | Five cards in suit bid and four cards in other major. |
| 1NT | 2C/3C or 3D | Forcing to game. Unbalanced hand with long minor and conceivably a four card major. |
| 1NT | 2C/3H or 3S | Slam try. Weak six card major. |
| 1NT | 2C/4C | Gerber. |
| 1NT | 2C/2NT | Four card major. 8-9. |
| 1NT | 2C/3NT | Four card major. 10-14. |
| 1NT | 2C/4NT | Four card major. 15-16. Not Blackwood. |
| 1NT | 2D | Transfer to two hearts. |
| 1NT | 2D/2NT, 3NT or 4NT | Same counts as above, only responder promises a five card heart suit. |
| 1NT | 2D/3H | Invitational. Six card heart suit. |
| 1NT | 2D/4H | Very mild slam try. |
| 1NT | 2D/3C or 3D | Two suiter. Forcing to game. |
| 1NT | 2H | Transfer to two spades. |
| 1NT | 2H/2NT, 3NT or 4NT | Same counts as above, only responder is promising five spades. |
| 1NT | 2H/3C or 3D | Two suiter. Forcing to game. |
| 1NT | 2H/3S | Invitational. Six card spade suit. |
| 1NT | 2H/4S | Very mild slam try. |
| 1NT | 2S | Minor suit Stayman. (See next page.) |
| 1NT | 2NT | 8-9 balanced. |
| 1NT | 3C, 3D | Invitational. |
| 1NT | 3H, 3S | Slam try with good six card suit. 13-15. |
| 1NT | 3NT | 10-14 balanced. |
| 1NT | 4C | Gerber. |
| 1NT | 4D | Transfer to four hearts. |
| 1NT | 4D/4NT | Blackwood. |
| 1NT | 4H | Transfer to four spades. |
| 1NT | 4H/4NT | Blackwood. |
| 1NT | 4NT | 15-16 balanced. |

## Some Minor Suit Stayman Sequences

| Opener | Responder | Meaning |
|---|---|---|
| 1NT<br>2NT | 2S | No four card minor. |
| 1NT<br>3C,3D | 2S | Four cards in the last bid suit. |
| 1NT<br>2NT | 2S<br>3C | Weak club/diamond two suiter does not wish to play in game. |
| 1NT<br>2NT or 3C | 2S<br>3D | A diamond signoff does not wish to play in game. |
| 1NT<br>2NT | 2S<br>3NT | 4-4-3-2 or 5-4-2-2 in the minors with 14-15 H.C.P. |
| 1NT<br>2NT,3C,3D | *2S<br>3H,3S | A minor game going two suiter with a singleton in the last bid suit. Be careful about no trump. |

*Responder can, if he wishes, treat his 5-4-3-1 minor two suiters as 5-5-2-1 hands and hope for the best.

| Opener | Responder | Opener | Responder |
|---|---|---|---|
| S. KJxx | S. Axx | 1NT | 2S |
| H. Axx | H. x | 3C | 3H |
| D. Ax | D. KQxxx | etc. | |
| C. KQxx | C. J10xx | | |

Opener will no longer play this hand in no trump once he discovers partner has a singleton heart.

23

## RESPONSES TO 2NT USING STAYMAN AND JACOBY TRANSFER

| Opener | Responder | Meaning |
|--------|-----------|---------|
| 2NT | 3C | Stayman. |
| 2NT | 3C/3H or 3S | Shows five cards in suit bid, and four cards in other major. |
| 2NT | 3C/3NT | At least one four card major. 5-10. |
| 2NT | 3C/4C | Gerber. |
| 2NT | 3C/4D | Slam try in diamonds. |
| 2NT | 3C/4H or 4S | Slam try in that major. Weak six card suit. |
| 2NT | 3C/4NT | At least one four card major. 11-12. Natural. |
| 2NT | 3D | Transfer to three hearts. |
| 2NT | 3D/3NT or 4NT | Five card heart suit and 5-10 to rebid 3NT and 11-12 to rebid 4NT. |
| 2NT | 3D/4C or 4D | Two suiter. Forcing. |
| 2NT | 3D/4H | Mild slam try. A 4D transfer can be used with a weaker hand. |
| 2NT | 3H | Transfer to 3S. |
| 2NT | 3H/3NT or 4NT | Five card spade suit and 5-10 to rebid 3NT and 11-12 to rebid 4NT. |
| 2NT | 3H/4C or 4D | Two suiter. Forcing. |
| 2NT | 3S | Minor suit Stayman with game forcing and slam hands only. |
| 2NT | 3NT | 5-10 balanced. |
| 2NT | 4C | Gerber. |
| 2NT | 4D | Transfer to four hearts. |
| 2NT | 4D/5C or 5D | Two suiter. Invitational to slam. |
| 2NT | 4D/4NT | Blackwood. |
| 2NT | 4H | Transfer to four spades. |
| 2NT | 4H/5C or 5D | Two suiter. Invitational to slam. |
| 2NT | 4H/4NT | Blackwood. |
| 2NT | 4NT | 11-12 balanced. Natural. |

## THE WEAK TWO BID

The "Weak Two Bid" is an opening bid of either two diamonds, two hearts, or two spades which describes a hand with a strong six card suit and typically 7-10 high card points.

It can be likened to an opening three bid except for the length of the suit.

Typical distributions are 6-3-3-1, 6-3-2-2 or 6-4-2-1. It is usually unwise to open a Weak Two with a void as partner is apt to misjudge both the offensive and defensive potential of the hand.

Also, it is unwise to open a Weak Two in diamonds with four cards in either major.

A good rule of thumb is to have three of the top five honor cards in your suit. However, suits that have 98 combinations need only two of the top five honors. Suits such as AQ98xx, AJ98xx, A1098xx, KJ98xx, QJ98xx are considered quite acceptable. It seldom pays to dip much lower in suit strength.

When playing Weak Two Bids, all game going hands as well as all no trump hands in the 22-24 range are opened with an artificial bid of two clubs. The opening bid of two no trump shows 20-21 or possibly 22 high card points. An opening bid of two clubs followed by a rebid of two no trump shows 22-23-24 high card points and a balanced hand. With 22 high card points, the player must judge whether to open two no trump or open two clubs and rebid two no trump. Usually if the hand is divided 4-3-3-3, it should be opened two no trump.

### Weak Two Bids in the Third Seat

Requirements are relaxed considerably for a Weak Two Bid in the third seat. Partner has passed and the main reason for the bid is usually lead direction. A Weak Two in the third seat can, therefore, be made with a good five card suit. Partner will seldom be strong enough to bid and if the opponents bid, the partner of the Weak Two bidder will know what to lead.

25

Examples of Weak Two spades bids in the third seat:

    (1) S. AKJ10x        (2) S. KQJxx        (3) S. KQ10xx
        H. xx                H. x                H. Axx
        D. Qxx               D. Kxxx             D. xx
        C. xxx               C. xxx              C. Jxx

Another advantage of playing Weak Two Bids is that they eliminate the need to open light in the third or fourth seat with a good suit and sub-minimum point count. Simply open two of your suit. It follows, therefore, when playing Weak Twos that if you open one of a suit in third or fourth seat and rebid your suit, you must have a full opening bid as you would have opened with a Weak Two if you did not.

## Responding to a Weak Two Bid

The partner of the Weak Two bidder must keep in mind that the opener has somewhere between 7-10 H.C.P. Therefore, if the responder is con-templating game on a misfit hand (a hand with a singleton in partner's long suit), he should have a minimum of 15-16 H.C.P. With less, he should PASS.

If partner opens 2H, pass with the following hands:

    (1) S. AJxx         (2) S. Kxxxx        (3) S. Q10xxxx
        H. x                H. x                H. x
        D. KQxx             D. AKQx             D. AKx
        C. QJxx             C. Qxx              C. KJx

With hands that have a doubleton in partner's suit the responder can be more aggressive; if he has a full opening bid with no wasted queens and jacks he should bid.

If partner opens 2H and you hold:

    (1) S. Axx          (2) S. AKQxxx       (3) S. xx
        H. xx               H. xx               H. xx
        D. AKxx             D. Axx              D. AKJ10xx
        C. Kxxx             C. xx               C. AKx

With (1) respond with a forcing bid of 2NT.

With (2) respond with a forcing bid of 2S.

With (3) respond with a forcing bid of 3D.

In other words, any new suit or 2NT is forcing in response to a Weak Two Bid. The Weak Two bidder will then either rebid his suit or jump to game in his suit (if he has a very strong suit) or raise to 3NT over 2NT or support your suit. He must bid again if the responder has not passed originally.

26

## Responding With a Fit in Partner's Suit

It is much easier to respond to a Weak Two with a fit. You have options, but mainly you will either raise to three preemptively, trying to keep the opponents out of the bidding, or raise to game which might also be preemptive or show a strong hand. Let the opponents worry about which it is. The Weak Two bidder is not allowed to bid over either raise!

Raise an opening bid of 2S to 3S with each of the following hands:

```
S.  Axx          S.  Qxx          S.  J10x
H.  xx           H.  Axxxx        H.  xx
D.  QJxxx        D.  x            D.  AQxxx
C.  xxx          C.  xxxx         C.  J10x
```

These preemptive raises are much more effective if your right hand opponent has passed.

Raise an opening bid of 2H to 4H with each of the following hands:

```
S.  x          S.  AKx          S.  Axxxx          S.  xxxx
H.  Axxx       H.  QJxx         H.  Axx            H.  KQxx
D.  KQxxx      D.  AQxx         D.  xx             D.  x
C.  xxx        C.  xx           C.  AQx            C.  Q10xx
```

There are other methods of responding to a Weak Two Bid than that described here. I feel that this one is simplest and probably the most accurate.

Many players use the response of 2NT as the only forcing response to a Weak Two and a response in a new suit can be passed. This method caters to the responding hand holding a long suit and a weak hand. However with that type of hand it is just as wise to pass the opening bid. Remember the opening bidder has a strong suit so nothing terrible can happen. If the opponents double you can always bid your long suit.

## Ogust Responses

Some experts use Ogust responses to a Weak Two Opening. Playing Ogust, responder, with an opening bid or better, bids 2NT and opener now describes his hand in a little more detail.

The responses to 2NT using Ogust are:

| | | |
|---|---|---|
| 3C | Bad suit | bad hand. |
| 3D | Good suit | bad hand. |
| 3H | Bad suit | good hand. |
| 3S | Good suit | good hand. |
| 3NT | Solid suit. | |

## Showing A Singleton

Another possibility is to show a singleton in response to 2NT. Opener shows any singleton he may hold. With no singleton opener rebids his suit with a minimum hand and bids 3NT with a maximum. This method is ideal for reaching some good slams.

| Opener | Responder | | Opener | Responder |
|---|---|---|---|---|
| S. AQ10xxx | S. KJx | | 2S | 2NT |
| H. x | H. xxxx | | 3H | 4NT |
| D. Qxx | D. A | | 5D | 6S |
| C. xxx | C. AKQxx | | Pass | |

Opener shows a singleton heart and responder checks for aces before bidding the laydown slam.

## Feature Showing

Many experts use feature showing rebids when responder bids 2NT:

| Opener | Responder | | Opener | Responder |
|---|---|---|---|---|
| S. KQ10xxx | S. Ax | | 2S | 2NT |
| H. xx | H. AQxx | | 3D | 3NT |
| D. Kxx | D. 10xx | | Pass | |
| C. xx | C. AQxx | | | |

Opener shows a feature in diamonds and responder elects to bid the no trump game. If opener had shown a feature in either hearts or clubs, responder would have bid the spade game.

## Defense to the Weak Two

The simplest defense is to assume the opening bid was one of a suit. If you are strong enough to double an opening 1S bid for takeout, you should double 2S for takeout. A direct overcall of 2NT shows 16-18 plus at least one stopper in the opponent's suit. An overcall in a suit shows either a strong five card major at the two level or a six card suit at the three level and the strength should be near that of an opening bid. If you have none of the requirements you should pass as your partner needs slightly less in the balancing position to compete. (See Weiss Convention.)

# LIMIT RAISES

A Limit Raise is a natural way of showing partner you have slightly more than a single raise. For example, if the bidding begins:

| North | East | South | West |
|-------|------|-------|------|
| 1S | Pass | 3S | |

South is NOT showing a game forcing raise with 13-16 support points. Instead South is describing a hand with four or five card support and 10-12 support points. The following hands would raise an opening 1S bid to 3S:

```
S. AJxx          S. KQxxx         S. Q10xx
H. xxx           H. xx            H. Axxx
D. AJxx          D. xxx           D. x
C. xx            C. AJx           C. J10xx
```

Limit Raises are used in all suits and in competition. The meaning never varies. Even if the player who makes the limit raise is a passed hand the bid carries the same meaning. Limit Raises in a minor suit typically show hands with five or even six card support. A Limit Raise is seldom given in a minor when holding a four card major.

The following hands raise an opening 1C bid to 3C:

```
S. xx            S. KQx           S. xx
H. xx            H. xxx           H. xx
D. Axx           D. xx            D. AJxx
C. KJxxxx        C. AJ10xx        C. KJ10xx
```

Limit Raises are a natural way of expressing these hands. A Limit Raise is not forcing. If opener is minimum, he passes with dispatch.

## What Does Responder do With Stronger Hands?

When playing Limit Raises and one picks up a hand in the 13-16 zone he must make some bid other than a jump raise, which is no longer forcing. There are many methods to handle these stronger hands. Here are a few:

## Singleton Swiss

Basically, hands that have four or more card major suit support will fall into three categories:

1. Balanced hands.  Hands with no singleton or void and no five or six card suit.

2. Hands with a singleton.  Usually 4-4-4-1 hands or 5-4-3-1 hands with five card support for opener's suit.

3. Hands that have a long side suit.

1. <u>The Balanced Hand</u>:  Partner opens 1S and you hold:

> S. AJxx
> H. xx
> D. KQxx
> C. Kxx

Jump to 2NT and over any bid partner makes bid 4S.  The opener never assumes that you have four card major support when you jump to 2NT.  However if you follow up your 2NT response with four of opener's major you show this type of hand.

| Opener | Responder |
|--------|-----------|
| 1H     | 2NT       |
| 3NT    | 4H        |

shows a four card heart support, a balanced hand and 13-16 support points.

2. Hands With a Singleton and 4-4-4-1 Distribution or 5-4-3-1 With Five Card Support:

These hands jump to four of the singleton suit!

| Opener | Responder | Opener | Responder |
|--------|-----------|--------|-----------|
| S. AJxxxx | S. KQxx | 1S | 4H! |
| H. Axx | H. x | 4NT | 5D |
| D. Kxx | D. QJ10x | 6S | Pass |
| C. x | C. AJxx | | |

Responder shows a singleton heart with primary spade support and 13-16 points.  An expert evaluator in the opener's seat would immediately envision a slam and check for aces.

When using this convention, a jump to 3S over an opening bid of 1H shows a singleton spade.  This is not the kind of convention you can forget and still recover.

Singleton Swiss can also be used over intervening bids:

| North | East | South | West |
|-------|------|-------|------|
| 1S    | 2D   | 4D    |      |

South is showing a singleton diamond with primary spade support.

3. <u>Hands With a Good Five or Any Six Card Side Suit</u>.

These hands bid the side suit and then jump to game in opener's major:

| Opener | Responder | Opener | Responder |
|--------|-----------|--------|-----------|
| S. AQxxx | S. KJxx | 1S | 2C |
| H. KQx | H. xx | 2D | 4S |
| D. Qxxx | D. x | Pass | |
| C. x | C. AQJxxx | | |

30

Responder shows a hand with a long club suit and four or five card spade support (almost always four). Opener needs aces in the red suits to contemplate a slam.

## Other Swiss Variations

Besides Singleton Swiss, there are a few other popular variations:

## Trump Honor Swiss

Jumps to four clubs or four diamonds in response to a major suit opening bid show 13-16 points but distinguish trump strength. A jump to four clubs shows zero or one of the top three honors and a jump to four diamonds two or three of the top three honors. Playing Inverted Trump Honor Swiss, four clubs shows the stronger trump holding and four diamonds the weaker.

Assuming the jump to 4C shows weaker trumps:

```
S. Jxxx
H. AKxx
D. xx
C. Axx
```

Respond 4C to an opening 1S bid, but 4D to an opening 1H bid.

## Control Swiss

Using this variation, there are five key controls, the four aces and the king of trump.

A response of 4C shows either one or two key controls.

A response of 4D shows three or four key controls.

It is also possible to reverse this and play 4C to show three or four controls and four diamonds one or two. Using the first variation:

```
S. Axxx
H. Kxxx
D. xx
C. AJx
```

respond 4C to an opening 1S bid (two controls), but 4D to an opening 1H bid (three controls).

In its simplest form Blackwood is a bid of 4NT which in certain sequences asks partner for aces. The responses are:

> 5C   shows zero or all four aces
> 5D   one ace
> 5H   two aces
> 5S   three aces

If the Blackwood bidder follows up the 4NT bid with 5NT he is asking for kings. The responses are:

> 6C   no kings
> 6D   one king
> 6H   two kings
> 6S   three kings
> 6NT  four kings

The 5NT bidder guarantees that all four aces are held by the partnership. The responder is allowed to jump to 7NT over 5NT rather than answer kings as, indeed, he must if he can count thirteen tricks.

| Opener | Responder | Opener | Responder |
| --- | --- | --- | --- |
| S. Kx | S. Axxx | 4H | 4NT |
| H. KQ10xxxxxx | H. A | 5C | 5NT |
| D. x | D. AJxx | 7H or 7NT | Pass |
| C. x | C. Axxx | | |

Responder asks for aces in order to tell the opener that he has all four aces. When the responder bids 5NT opener now knows that responder has all the aces. Knowing this he leaps to 7H or 7NT with equal safety.

## Responding to Blackwood With a Void

There are two popular methods. Blackwood himself suggests this:

With no aces and a void respond 6C

With one ace and void respond 6D

With two aces and a void respond 6H

With three aces and a void respond 6S

Partner must be able to figure out from your previous bidding in which suit you are void. This is not always so easy to do. Blackwood says you should only show the void in this manner if you are sure your partner can identify the suit. Also you would not show a void in any suit in which your partner has shown particular strength.

## Roman Blackwood With a Void

The alternate method of showing a void is Roman Blackwood which pinpoints the void suit. Responses are as follows:

With no aces and a void simply respond 5C.

With one ace and a void jump to six of the void suit if it is lower ranking than the trump suit.

With one ace and a void jump to six of the trump suit if the void is higher ranking than the trump suit.

With two aces and a void respond 5NT.

With three aces and a void respond 5D (if the agreed suit is not diamonds). Then when opener signs off at five of a major bid six of your void suit if it is lower than the trump suit or raise to six of the agreed suit if the void is higher ranking.

## Blackwood Over Interference

Assume the bidding proceeds:

| North | East | South | West |
|-------|------|-------|------|
| 1H    | 3D   | 3S    | 4D   |
| 4S    | Pass | 4NT   | 5D   |
| ?     |      |       |      |

How does North show aces after the intervening 5D bid? Again, there is a difference of opinion. Blackwood says that the responses should be as follows:

Double: Either shows no aces or a hand which contains an ace

but is unusually well suited to defense.

The next suit, in this case 5H, shows one ace.

The next suit, 5S, shows two aces, etc.

## DOPI

Many experts use the convention "DOPI" over interference. This is easy to remember because the "D" stands for double and the "P" for Pass. Therefore, a double shows no (0) aces, a pass one (1) ace and the next ranking suit, two (2) aces.

# DEPO

For interference at the six or seven level "DEPO" is clearly best. Now a double shows an even number of aces (zero or two) and a pass shows an odd number of aces (one or three).

Playing "DEPO" if the bidding proceeds as follows:

| South | West | North | East |
|-------|------|-------|------|
| 1S | Pass | 3S | 4D |
| 4NT. | 6D! | Pass | |

North's pass shows an odd number of aces. Had North doubled 6D he would be showing an even number of aces. The advantage of this convention is that the responder need never commit himself with a bid at the six level which might put the partnership too high. Instead he shows his aces quite eloquently by either doubling or passing.

## How to Get Out at 5NT

Sometimes you find after asking for aces that you are missing two aces but are already beyond your trump suit at the five level. Your only chance for a plus is to play the hand in 5NT. But if you bid 5NT partner will answer kings. The solution is to bid five of an unbid major which forces partner to bid 5NT.

| Opener | Responder | | Opener | Responder |
|--------|-----------|--|--------|-----------|
| S. KQx | S. xx | | 1C | 1H |
| H. Kx | H. AQJx | | 3C | 4C |
| D. Kx | D. xxx | | 4NT | 5D |
| C. AKJ10xx | C. Qxxx | | 5S | 5NT |
| | | | Pass | |

Opener has not bid very well but what else is new? He should be very careful about using Blackwood when clubs is the agreed suit and he holds only one ace. It is almost a no-no. In any event, when responder shows only one ace the most likely spot for the hand is 5NT. Opener now bids five of a major compelling the responder to bid 5NT which the opener passes. Phew!

34

## Key Card Blackwood

In this variation, the king of trumps is counted as an ace and therefore there are five aces instead of four. When using Key Card Blackwood, the responses to 4NT are:

    5C    shows either no aces or four aces.
    5D    shows either one ace or five aces.
    5H    shows two aces.
    5S    shows three aces.

A subsequent bid of 5NT asks for kings not counting the king of trump.

One problem when using this convention is that both players must know whether or not a suit has been agreed upon and in the case of double agreement which is the agreed suit. An improved variation to these responses has been suggested, but is is slightly more complicated.

    5C    shows zero or three aces.
    5D    shows one or four aces.
    5H    shows two or five aces and denies the queen of trump.
    5S    shows two aces and promises the queen of trump.

Using this method, you can determine whether or not your partner has the queen of trump if he responds either 5H or 5S.

A further extension is to ask your partner if he has the queen of trumps if his response is either 5C or 5D. This is done by bidding the next ranking suit, excluding trumps. The negative response is the next suit and the positive response is to skip a suit. Example:

| Opener | Responder | Opener | Responder |
|--------|-----------|--------|-----------|
| S. Axxxxx | S. Kxx | 2C | 2D |
| H. AKQJx | H. xx | 2S | 3S |
| D. A | D. Kxxxx | 4NT | 5D |
| C. A | C. Jxx | 5H | 5S |
|  |  | 6S | Pass |

Opener begins with an artificial 2C and then after bidding spades receives support. 4NT is Key Card Blackwood and responder shows one or four aces. Opener knows that responder has the king of spades and inquires about the queen by bidding 5H. Responder denies the queen by bidding 5S. If responder has the queen of spades his proper response is 5NT in which case the opener can safely bid 7S.

## When Not to Use Blackwood

In general Blackwood should not be used by a player who holds a void suit or two or more losers in an unbid suit.  Cue bidding works out best in these cases.

| Opener | Responder | | Opener | Responder |
|--------|-----------|--|--------|-----------|
| S. AKQxxx | S. J10xx | | 2C | 2D |
| H. KQx | H. Ax | | 2S | 3S |
| D. None | D. QJxx | | 4C | 4H |
| C. AKQx | C. xxx | | 7S | |

Opener cue bids his club control and responder his heart control.  Opener can now safely bid seven.  Blackwood would be worthless here as opener would not know which ace responder held.

## When is 4NT Blackwood?

This one has caused experts trouble since time immemorial.  Here are a few simple rules:

> After any suit agreement, 4NT is Blackwood.

> If no suit has been bid, 4NT is not Blackwood.

> If Gerber is being used by the partnership any sequence in which 4C would ask for aces automatically means that 4NT is not Blackwood.

> Overcalls of opening four bids with 4NT are not Blackwood.

> If both opponents show strength and partner has not bid, 4NT is not Blackwood but the Unusual No Trump.

| South | West | North | East |
|-------|------|-------|------|
| 1S | Pass | 3S | 4NT |

(East's 4NT bid is for the minors, not Blackwood.)

If Gerber is not being used the partnership must decide upon the use of 4NT in questionable sequences such as:

| Opener | Responder |
|--------|-----------|
| 1H | 2NT |
| 4NT? | |

Is this Blackwood?  Playing Gerber it is not as a leap to 4C would ask for aces.  But not playing Gerber how else can the opener ask for aces?  On the other hand how can the opener raise to 4NT naturally if every 4NT bid is to be considered Blackwood?

Problems, problems, problems.

# THE WEAK JUMP OVERCALL

The Weak Junp Overcall is a very popular convention, particularly in tournament play.  It can be likened to a Weak Two Bid.

Its salient features are a good six card suit and typically 7-9/10 H.C.P. A Weak Jump Overcall skips over exactly one level of bidding.  A Weak Jump Overcall at the three level is apt to contain a seven card suit vulnerable.

Assuming right hand opponent opens the bidding with 1C, the following hands overcall 2S, weak:

|  | (1) | (2) | (3) |
|---|---|---|---|
| S. | AQJ874 | KJ10876 | QJ10876 |
| H. | 54 | A3 | 5 |
| D. | 765 | 87 | KJ76 |
| C. | 54 | 1076 | 76 |

The problem that arises with Weak Jump Overcalls is mainly how to handle stronger hands with six cards suits - hands which have good six card suits. and 12-14 H.C.P.

For example, assume your right hand opponent opens 1C and you have each of the following hands:

|  | (1) | (2) | (3) |
|---|---|---|---|
| S. | AKJ987 | 2 | 6 |
| H. | A109 | KQJ987 | KJ10 |
| D. | 65 | AQ10 | AKQ876 |
| C. | 54 | 876 | 976 |

Each of these is a nice Intermediate Jump Overcall.  As you can't have your cake and eat it, you must learn how to handle these hands when playing Weak Jump Overcalls.

The most common treatment is to overcall at the one level if possible, and if you get a chance rebid your suit at the two level.  As it is unusual for a player who makes a simple overcall to repeat his overcall the reason will be obvious.  You have an Intermediate Jump Overcall and are playing Weak Jump Overcalls!

| East | South | West | North |
|---|---|---|---|
| 1C | 1H | 1S | Pass |
| 2D | 2H | | |

South has an Intermediate Jump Overcall in hearts, similar to hand (2). The real problem arises when it becomes necessary to make your rebid at the three level.  Then it is a question of vulnerability and how much strength the opponents have shown from their bidding.

Assume you have a hand like this:
S. 87
H. AK9876
D. AQ4
C. 65

Neither side is vulnerable and the bidding proceeds:

| East | South (you) | West | North |
|------|-------------|------|-------|
| 1C   | 1H          | 2NT  | Pass  |
| 3C   | ?           |      |       |

Although it is true that you have a nice hand and have that "left-over feeling," it is obviously pointless to rebid your suit in the face of the East-West bidding sequence. Play it cool and PASS!

| East | South (you) | West | North |
|------|-------------|------|-------|
| 1C   | 1H          | 2C   | Pass  |
| 3C   | ?           |      |       |

Now there is more logic to repeating the overcall at the three level. The general rule therefore is this: When you have a stronger overcall (good six card suit and 12-14 H.C.P.), make a simple overcall at the one or two level and if the opponents have shown little or no indication of extra strength repeat your overcall at the two level, if possible. But be careful about repeating your overcall at the three level unless your suit has good intermediate cards.

Of course, we are assuming all this time that your partner is passing. Naturally if your partner bids a suit or helps your suit you can take more aggressive action.

### The Weak Jump Overcall at the Three Level

This overcall usually has a paralyzing effect on all but the most experienced opposition.

To repeat, a Weak Jump Overcall skips over exactly one level of bidding.

| East | South |
|------|-------|
| 1C   | 3D    |

South is technically not making a Weak Jump Overcall because he is skipping over two levels of bidding. South is making a preemptive overcall which is similar to an opening three bid. Everyone plays this as pre-emptive.

However, if the bidding proceeds:

| East | South |
|------|-------|
| 1D   | 3C    |

not everyone plays this as preemptive or weak. This is a Weak Jump Overcall by prior agreement. If using Weak Jump Overcalls, South's hand will
be very similar to an opening three bid but is apt to have a six instead
of a seven card suit, particularly at favorable vulnerability.

South might have any of these hands for the 3C bid:

| (1) S. 5 | (2) S. K8 | (3) S. 976 |
|----------|-----------|------------|
| H. K5 | H. 2 | H. QJ8 |
| D. Q76 | D. K743 | D. 2 |
| C. KJ108754 | C. QJ10543 | C. KQJ1087 |

Notice that a Weak Jump Overcall seldom has as many as two defensive
tricks. Indeed, when considering a penalty double, the most you should
count on from your partner is one defensive trick after he has made a Weak
Jump Overcall.

## Responses to Weak Jump Overcalls

Every so often the partner of the Weak Jump overcaller has a good hand.
Here is a list of possible responses to a Weak Jump Overcall and their
meanings. Take a sample sequence:

| East | South | West | North |
|------|-------|------|-------|
| 1C   | 2H    | Pass | ?     |

If North bids a new suit, 2S or 3D, that is not forcing but with support
South should raise. Bridge is a game in which it does not pay to conceal
support.

If North jumps in a new suit, that is highly invitational and South makes
every effort to raise North to game with a suitable hand. However some
Weak Jump Overcalls are not much suitable for anything.

If North bids 2NT that is invitational and shows about 15-17 points. A
jump to 3NT is the end.

A raise to three of the overcaller's suit is preemptive and South is
barred from further bidding. A raise to four is a two-edged sword. It

may either be a further preempt or North may have a very good hand.  In
any case South need not worry, he always passes.  If the opponents compete
South allows North to take charge.

If North absolutely wants to force the bidding his only forcing response
is a cue bid of the opponent's suit, in this case 3C.  South will then at-
tempt to describe his hand by either showing a secondary four card suit,
bidding no trump with a club stopper, or rebidding his original suit, jumping to four if his suit is unusually strong.  If north cue bids 3C and then
bids a new suit that is a one round force.  If North cue bids and then bids
3NT South has the option of returning to his original suit - an option he
did not have if North had leaped directly to 3NT.

## Conclusion

Weak Jump Overcalls are very effective weapons when not misused.  They
should not be so weak that you would be afraid to put the hand down as
dummy for fear the whole table will laugh.  Weak Jump Overcalls have typically 7-9/10 H.C.P. with a good six card suit at the two level, and either
a six or seven card suit at the three level (more likely seven vulnerable).
Remember the opponents are allowed to double.

When holding stronger one suited hands, 12-14 H.C.P., it usually pays to
make a simple overcall and then repeat the overcall if possible at the two
level.  If the opponents force you to repeat the overcall at the three
level be sure you know what you are doing, otherwise a blood bath may ensue.

The Intermediate Jump Overcall (I.J.O.) is used to describe hands that have good six card suits with twelve to fourteen high card points. An I.J.O. at the three level may have a seven card suit with a slightly higher point count.

The advantage of this bid is that it liberates the takeout double to describe balanced hands - and not one suited hands in this point range. It also has the effect of describing the hand to partner in one bid rather than making a simple overcall and then overcalling again at a higher, riskier level to emphasize the strength of your hand.

Assume you hold the following hand with neither side vulnerable:

S. 2     H. AKJ986     D. AJ9     C. 765

You are South and the bidding proceeds:

| East | South |
|------|-------|
| 1C   | ?     |

What should you bid? Playing I.J.O.'s South has a simple two heart call, describing the hand in one bid and leaving the rest to partner. A one heart overcall would hardly do justice to the hand and a double would run the risk of hearing partner bid spades for all eternity.

An I.J.O. at the three level (usually three of a minor over one of a major) is invitational to three no trump, has on the average thirteen to fifteen high card points and has at least seven quick tricks for no trump purposes.

This time South holds:

S. 54     H. A76     D. 65     C. AKQJ98

The bidding proceeds:

| East | South |
|------|-------|
| 1S   | ?     |

South overcalls three clubs, not two clubs, to describe this hand and hopes partner can scrape up three no trump with a spade stopper and one outside trick.

# Responding to an I.J.O.

Any new suit is forcing and a single raise or 2NT is invitational. Do not respond to an I.J.O with a weak hand. It takes a little less than an opening bid (ten or more points) to smell game. With less it pays to pass.

Assume the bidding proceeds:

| East | South | West | North |
|------|-------|------|-------|
| 1C | 2H | Pass | ? |

What should North bid with each of the following hands?

| (1) | S. Q98765 | (2) | S. AJ5 | (3) | S. A5 | (4) | S. A4 |
|-----|-----------|-----|--------|-----|-------|-----|-------|
| | H. None | | H. 54 | | H. 876 | | H. 987 |
| | D. K76 | | D. 10987 | | D. A8765 | | D. AQ1087 |
| | C. K987 | | C. KJ87 | | C. J54 | | C. 654 |

With (1)   Pass.

With (2)   Bid 2NT.   Invitational, showing 9-10 high card points.

With (3)   Bid 3H.   Invitational.

With (4)   Bid 4H.   Your hand is worth eleven points in support of hearts and partner's hand is usually worth about fifteen points (counting everything) so you are in range.

The Unusual No Trump is a convention designed to show two suited hands with one bid. As with all conventions, confusion arises unless both partners realize when a no trump overcall is unusual, showing a two suiter, and when it has its natural meaning, a balanced hand with a fixed count.

In order to facilitate a difficult subject we begin by analyzing no trump overcalls by a <u>passed</u> hand.

For example:

| South | West | North | East |
|-------|------|-------|------|
| Pass  | Pass | Pass  | 1H   |
| 1NT   |      |       |      |

What can South mean? Conventionally a direct 1NT overcall by a <u>passed</u> hand is always "unusual" in that it shows the "lower two unbid suits." A typical hand might be: S. K4   H. 3   D. A8765   C. Q10876

It might be wise to point out that a direct 1NT overcall by a passed hand logically shows a two suiter as it is foolish to come wandering into the bidding with a balanced hand of less than 13 points after partner has already passed.

How distributional should the one no trump overcaller be? In cases of direct overcalls the distribution should be 5-5 or possibly 6-5. Not 5-4!

What does a direct 2NT overcall by a passed hand mean?

| South | West | North | East |
|-------|------|-------|------|
| Pass  | Pass | Pass  | 1S   |
| *2NT  |      |       |      |

As South could have used a 1NT overcall to describe a fairly normal two-suited minor hand, a 2NT overcall shows even more distribution and playing strength. Keep in mind we are discussing <u>passed</u> hands. A possible hand might be: S. 4   H. 3   D. KQ986   C. KJ10876

*Alternatively 2NT over 1S can be used to show a red two suiter, and over 1H to show spades and diamonds (in other words, the two higher ranking unbid suits).

You may have noticed that in both examples South bids no trump over a major suit opening and is, therefore, showing the minors. What if South overcalls one or two no trump over a minor?

| South | West | North | East |
|-------|------|-------|------|
| Pass  | Pass | Pass  | 1D   |
| 1NT   |      |       |      |

South is showing the two lower-ranking unbid suits. In this case, clubs and hearts. A possible hand might be:   S. 4   H. A8764   D. 54   C. KQ873
If South overcalls 2NT he is still showing clubs and hearts but is more distributional.

We are now able to state a rule about no trump overcalls by passed hands:

> ANY DIRECT OVERCALL OF ONE OR TWO NO TRUMP BY A PASSED HAND IS
> "UNUSUAL" AND SHOWS THE TWO LOWER RANKING UNBID SUITS.  THE DIS-
> TRIBUTION WILL ALMOST ALWAYS BE 5-5 or 6-5.

Another way of stating this: over a major suit the direct overcall of 1NT or 2NT shows both minors;  over a minor suit the direct overcall of 1NT or 2NT shows hearts and the other minor.

Notice that the word "direct" is underlined. Why? Because there is a difference between a direct overcall of 1NT and a balancing or reopening bid of 1NT. Consider this bidding sequence:

| South | West | North | East |
|-------|------|-------|------|
| Pass  | 1H   | Pass  | Pass |
| 1NT   |      |       |      |

Notice that South has not made a direct overcall of 1NT but rather a re-opening bid of 1NT. Reopening bids of 1NT are never unusual and when made by a passed hand show 10-12 high card points with at least one stopper in the opponent's suit. The range for a non-passed hand is 11-15. South might have:   S. A76   H. KJ8   D. QJ87   C. J106

Had South something like:   S. K4   H. 3   D. A8765   C. QJ986, he must reopen with 2NT. Reopening bids of 2NT by a passed hand are unusual and show the two lower unbid suits. The distribution can be 5-4 if the opponents have found a fit -- otherwise 5-5 or 6-5.

| East | South | West | North |
|------|-------|------|-------|
| 1H   | Pass  | 2H   | Pass  |
| Pass | 2NT   |      |       |

South might have:   S. K4   H. 62   D. KJ98   C. A10972

Another common position that a passed hand encounters is:

| South | West | North | East |
|-------|------|-------|------|
| Pass  | Pass | Pass  | 1H   |
| Pass  | 1S   | Pass  | Pass |
| ?     |      |       |      |

Let's give South two possible hands:

    (1)   S. AQ3   H. KJ98   D. Q54   C. 765

    (2)   S. 65   H. 54   D. AJ98   C. KJ1087

With hand (1) South bids 1NT.  All reopening 1NT bids are natural.

With hand (2) South doubles.  A reopening double is used with length and strength in the two unbid suits.

To repeat: When the opponents have bid two suits a passed hand can enter the bidding with either a direct no trump overcall or a double.  Double shows less distribtuion and more defense.  Another position:

| South | West | North | East |
|-------|------|-------|------|
| Pass  | 1H   | Pass  | 2H   |
| 2NT?  |      |       |      |

South should have something like:   S. 5   H. A3   D. Q10932   C. QJ965

Any overcall of 2NT by a passed hand is "unusual."

We are now in a position to summarize overcalls in no trump made by a passed hand:

    ALL NO TRUMP OVERCALLS BY A PASSED HAND, WITH THE EXCEPTION OF THE

    REOPENING BID OF 1NT, ARE UNUSUAL AND SHOW THE TWO LOWER RANKING

    UNBID SUITS IF THE OPPONENTS HAVE BID ONE SUIT, OR THE TWO UNBID

    SUITS IF THE OPPONENTS HAVE BID TWO SUITS.

We now leave the passed hand and discuss no trump overcalls by a non-passed hand.

The most common, of course, is:

| East | South | West | North |
|------|-------|------|-------|
| 1S   | 1NT?  |      |       |

The direct overcall of 1NT by a non-passed hand is natural and shows 16-18 points with at least one stopper in the opponent's suit.

In the balancing position it shows typically 12-14.

| West | North | East | South |
|------|-------|------|-------|
| 1H   | Pass  | Pass | 1NT   |

South has 11/12-15 HIGH COUNT POINTS. With more he doubles and then bids no trump. (North assumes 12-14 although the range in theory is 11-15.)

Next we have the direct overcall of 2NT:

| East | South | West | North |
|------|-------|------|-------|
| 1S   | 2NT?  |      |       |

Most experts now use this bid to show the two lower ranking unbid suits (the minors over a major), and it is therefore, unusual. When a 2NT overcall is made by a non-passed hand it should show 10-13 points in high cards with at least 5-5 in the two suits. A possible South hand:

S. 4   H. KQ   D. AJ876   C. K9876

It must be pointed out here that the Unusual No Trump overcall is not a toy and should not be used every time you have 5-5 in the two lower ranking unbid suits. You should have nearly two defensive tricks if you have not passed originally.

If you make the bid indiscriminately, partner will never know whether or not to sacrifice and you will have destroyed the original purpose of the bid which was to show a "decent" two suited hand without risking getting beyond the level of three. Bear in mind that if the opponents buy the hand after an Unusual No Trump overcall declarer has a very clear picture of the distri-bution which will help him greatly in the play. Therefore, you should have some idea of buying the hand when you use the bid.

The next two sequences have been the subject of much discussion:

| (1) West | North | East | South |
|----------|-------|------|-------|
| 1S       | Pass  | 2S   | 2NT?  |

Is this the Unusual No Trump? Or does it simply show an 18-20 point balanced hand? A good case could be made for either. East could be very light for his raise and South might well have a strong hand. Alternately, what is

South to do with both minors? This is a ticklish situation and must be decided within the partnership. On balance South figures to have a minor two-suiter more often than a blockbuster with both opponents bidding.

| (2) | West | North | East | South |
|-----|------|-------|------|-------|
|     | 1S   | Pass  | 2D   | 2NT?  |

What is South doing here? This sequence is a little different. Both opponents have shown good hands so it is unlikely that South could have a hand strong enough to really want to say 2NT naturally. Here it is clearly better played as "unusual" for the two unbid suits. Why doesn't South double if he has the two unbid suits?

In cases where there is a choice between doubling and using the Unusual No Trump, both of which convey length in the unbid suits, the Unusual No Trump is used to show a more unbalanced hand (a weak freak) with less defensive strength and the double is used to show a more balanced hand with more defensive strength.

If South has: S. 4   H. KJ8765   D. 4   C. KQ765, he says 2NT. However, if South has: S. A43   H. AK87   D. 4   C. QJ876, he doubles. You have this choice only when the opponents have bid two suits.

Another touchy sequence:

| (3) | West | North | East | South |
|-----|------|-------|------|-------|
|     | 1H   | Pass  | 1S   | 2NT?  |

What is South doing? First, let's be sure we know what South would mean had he simply overcalled 1NT. That would be natural. Here again, although South could have a huge hand it is wiser to play the jump to 2NT as unusual.

Let's see if we can form any general rules for no trump overcalls made by non-passed hands.

ANY DIRECT OVERCALL OF 1NT MADE BY A NON-PASSED HAND IS NATURAL AND SHOWS 16-18 HIGH CARD POINTS. ANY DIRECT OVERCALL OF 2NT BY A NON-PASSED HAND IS UNUSUAL AND SHOWS THE TWO LOWER RANKING UNBID SUITS.

We have thus far confined our discussion to overcalls of no trump at the one or two level. However, the Unusual No Trump overcall is frequently used at higher levels where the meaning is far more obvious.

Take these examples:

| West | North | East | South |
|------|-------|------|-------|
| 1H | Pass | 3H | 3NT? |

Certainly South will not have a hand strong enough to wish to play 3NT against opponents who are bidding strongly. This is the Unusual No Trump asking for a choice in the two lower unbid suits (clubs and diamonds).

Or this:

| West | North | East | South |
|------|-------|------|-------|
| 1S | Pass | 4S | 4NT? |

Once again South is showing a terrific two suited hand. North is to assume that it is a club-diamond two-suiter. However, if North bids 5C and South bids 5D, South is showing a red two-suiter. The level makes it impossible for South unless this flexibility exists.

This makes it necessary to form another rule. When the opponents have bid two suits, the Unusual No Trump guarantees the other two suits. However, when the opponents have bid one suit up to the three or four level a no trump over-call shows a freak two-suiter. Any two suits! (But partner assumes the lower two.) This may sound confusing, so an example:

| West | North | East | South |
|------|-------|------|-------|
| 1S | Pass | 4S | 4NT |

South may have: S. Void   H. 54   D. KQ876   C. AQ10986, in which case he will pass any response that North makes. Or South may have: S. Void H. KJ876   D. AK8764   C. 54, in which case he will bid 5D over partner's 5C to show that his Unusual No Trump bid was based on diamonds and hearts. Or with: S. 3   H. AQJ987   D. 5   C. AK1095, if partner bids 5D, South bids 5H to show hearts and clubs.

Incidentally, if you can't remember all of this, relax....nobody else can either!

## Responding to the Unusual No Trump

Rather than memorizing a list of rules for responding to the Unusual No Trump, try to visualize partner's hand. You should see two long suits. If you fit one of those suits and have as little as an ace on the outside you are close to game!

For example - sitting South, you hold:  S. A543  H. 432  D. AJ876  C. 10

The bidding proceeds:

| West | North | East | South |
|------|-------|------|-------|
| 1H   | 2NT   | Pass | ?     |

Your partner has forced you to select one of his minor suits.  You would be obliged to do this with three small cards in one suit and two small cards in the other.  But look at what you have.  Your correct bid is 5D.  Remember, partner has never passed and should have a reasonable two suiter.

Let's say you have this hand on the same bidding:  S. QJ984  H. Q765  D. 765  C. 4 - now your proper bid is 3D and you should be grateful that you have three cards in one of partner's suits.  Remember you are not bidding diamonds, you are supporting partner in diamonds.  Once in a great while you can even raise to 3NT!  Of course you must be quite strong in the majors.  Let's say you have S. AK7  H. AQJ87  D. Q76  C. 87 and your partner overcalls an opening 1H bid to your left with 2NT.  Bid 3NT.  In order to do this you should have a sound opening bid with double stoppers in partner's short suits.

Most important to bear in mind is that for practical purposes you are the captain.  Partner has already forced you to pick one of his suits at the three level and you must take charge if you have a good fit.

Your right hand opponent may double partner's Unusual No Trump bid.  What should you do then?

| West | North | East | South |
|------|-------|------|-------|
| 1H   | 2NT   | Dbl. | ?     |

You hold:  (1) S. AJxxx   H. Jxxx   D. x    C. Jxx
           (2) S. KQxxx   H. Jxxx   D. xx   C. xx

(1) Bid 3C to prevent partner from bidding 3D, which he might do if you pass.
(2) Pass and let partner escape to his longer minor.

By bidding over the double you are saying that you definitely prefer one of partner's suits.

Now a short quiz on the Unusual No Trump.

I. You are South and East, to your right, opens 1H.  What do you bid on each of the following hands?

```
(1) S. AJ8        (2) S. 76         (3) S. AK8        (4) S. 76
    H. KJ87           H. 2              H. AK87           H. 76
    D. Q76            D. KQ876          D. A76            D. AJ876
    C. KQ8            C. AQ1086         C. KJ8            C. KQ87
```

Answers

(1) 1NT.  You are not a passed hand so this bid shows 16-18 points and a
          balanced hand.

(2) 2NT.  The Unusual No Trump for the minors over a major.

(3) Dbl.  Using the Unusual No Trump, double and then jump in no trump with
          20 points.

(4) Pass. You do not have the proper distribution for a 2NT overcall and
          your hand does not warrant a two diamond overcall.  If West raises
          to 2H and the bidding comes back to you, you might balance with
          2NT (unusual, for the minors).


II.  This time you are South but the bidding has proceeded as follows:

        West     North     East     South

        1H       2NT       Pass     ?


What do you bid with the following South hands?

```
(1)              (2)              (3)              (4)              (5)              (6)

S. A76           S. AQJ10876      S. 7654          S. KJ1087        S. KQ8           S. J8765
H. K8765         H. 43            H. A3            H. KQ1093        H. AKJ8          H. K7654
D. 1076          D. K5            D. KJ108         D. 4             D. K87           D. 2
C. 43            C. 43            C. 543           C. 54            C. 543           C. Q4
```

Answers

(1) 3D.   You have been asked to select a minor and that's what you are doing.

(2) 4S.   You are allowed to over-rule partner with a suit like this.

(3) 4D.   Inviting game in diamonds.

(4) Pass. Showing strength in both majors but not enough to bid 3NT.

(5) 3NT.  No comment.

(6) 3C.   It is not for you to reason why, it is for you to do or die!
          Obviously, the 2NT bidder should not do too much more bidding
          when responder simply selects one of his suits without jumping.
          He usually passes.

A common error to avoid is first making an Unusual No Trump overcall forcing

partner to pick one of your suits and then persisting in raising him because

you have five cards in the suit he picked!

You told him that when you made your no trump overcall.  It is up to the

partner to take a sacrifice not the Unusual No Trump bidder.  He has already

told his story and no one likes to hear the same story twice.

Partner opens one club and you hold:

```
(1)  S. xx           (2)  S. xx           (3)  S. xx
     H. KQxxxx             H. AQ10xxx           H. KQxxxx
     D. J10x              D. Axx               D. AK
     C. xx                C. xx                C. J10x
```

With each of these hands you respond 1H; partner rebids 1NT.

With (1): You bid two hearts, fully expecting partner to pass.

With (2): You obviously can't sign off at 2H, so you jump to 3H.  Is this forcing?  Assume for the moment that it is simply invitational, so you invite by rebidding 3H.

Now we must deal with (3).  If a jump to 3H is invitational, how can you force with (3)?  You could leap to 4H or 3NT, or perhaps jump to 3C, assuming that this is forcing; but the direct jumps to game are unilateral decisions, and the jump to 3C is misleading.

Perhaps you play the jump rebid to 3H as forcing, so you have no trouble with the third hand.  But what do you rebid with the second one?  The answer to this recurring misery is that <u>the</u> <u>system</u> <u>is</u> <u>not</u> <u>playable</u>.  And this is one of the most common of all bidding sequences.

Try these:

```
(1)  S. xx           (2)  S. xx           (3)  S. xx
     H. Axxxx             H. AKxxx             H. AKxxx
     D. Q10xx             D. QJ10x             D. QJ10x
     C. xx                C. xx                C. Ax
```

This time, your partner opens 1D, you respond 1H, and partner rebids 1NT.

With (1): You rebid two diamonds, expecting a pass.

With (2): If you play 3D as invitational, that would seem to be best.

With (3): You are in trouble if you play 3D as invitational, as you are too strong, and are almost forced into rebidding 3NT, or something even crazier (such as 3C) to create a forcing situation.

Perhaps you play the jump to 3D as forcing in this sequence.  Fine.  But now what do you do with your invitational hand, such as (2)?  Certainly you can't bid a loud 2D with (2) and a soft 2D with (1).  Can't you see?  <u>The</u> <u>system</u> <u>is</u> <u>unplayable</u>.

How about two-suited responding hands?

```
(1)  S. x              (2)  S. x              (3)  S. x
     H. Kxxxx               H. AJ10xx              H. AKxxx
     D. QJ10xx              D. KQxxx               D. AQ10xx
     C. xx                  C. xx                  C. xx
```

Partner opens 1C and you respond 1H.  Now you hear 1NT.

With (1): You rebid 2D, which is considered a signoff by most after a 1NT
rebid.  If you and your partner play 2D as forcing, you probably have to
rebid 2H.  Good luck!

With (2): If 2D is a signoff, you would like to invite game by jumping to
3D.  Oh no, a jump is forcing.  So you can't invite game.  So what do you do?
If 3D is forcing and 2D is a signoff, the best thing to do is never to get
dealt this particular hand.

Of course, if you decide to play 3D as invitational, you are in stormy waters
if you pick up (3).  Now you would like to force with 3D.  Apparently you
can't have your cake and eat it too.

Playing this intolerable method, you can't sign off, invite and force over
1NT.  You must give up one of them.  Who wants to play such a method?  I
don't, you don't, nobody does.

The answer is to junk that archaic method and play something that allows you
to show all three types of hand over a 1NT rebid.

For some years a few experts have adopted and played variations of what I am
about to propose.  This is the rule:
AFTER A 1NT REBID BY OPENER, A 2C REBID BY RESPONDER CREATES A FORCING SITUA-
TION.  IF THE RESPONDER DOES NOT REBID 2C, HIS JUMP SUIT-REBIDS ARE INVITA-
TIONAL, WHILE HIS SIMPLE SUIT-REBIDS ARE SIGNOFFS.

Now let's go back to our first set of three responding hands:

```
(1)  S. xx             (2)  S. xx             (3)  S. xx
     H. KQxxxx              H. AQ10xxx             H. KQxxxx
     D. J10x                D. Axx                 D. AK
     C. xx                  C. xx                  C. J10x
```

| Opener | Responder | |
|--------|-----------|--|
| 1C     | 1H        | |
| 1NT    | 2H        | Signoff - Hand (1). |
|        | 3H        | Invitational - Hand (2). |
|        | 2C        | To be followed by 3H; forcing to game - Hand (3). |

IF, AFTER REBIDDING TWO CLUBS, RESPONDER THEN BIDS A NEW SUIT, JUMPS, OR SUPPORTS OPENER'S FIRST-BID SUIT, HE CREATES A GAME FORCE.

Using this rule, we have no trouble with the second batch of hands either.

| (1) | S. xx<br>H. Axxxx<br>D. Q10xx<br>C. xx | (2) | S. xx<br>H. AKxxx<br>D. QJ10x<br>C. xx | (3) | S. xx<br>H. AKxxx<br>D. QJxx<br>C. Ax |
|---|---|---|---|---|---|

| Opener | Responder | |
|---|---|---|
| 1D | 1H | |
| 1NT | 2D | Signoff - hand (1). |
| | 3D | Invitational - hand (2). |
| | 2C | To be followed by 3D; forcing to game - hand (3). |

Nor with the two-suited hands:

| (1) | S. x<br>H. Kxxxx<br>D. QJ10xx<br>C. xx | (2) | S. x<br>H. AJ10xx<br>D. KQxxx<br>C. xx | (3) | S. x<br>H. AKxxx<br>D. AQ10xx<br>C. xx |
|---|---|---|---|---|---|

| Opener | Responder | |
|---|---|---|
| 1C | 1H | |
| 1NT | 2D | Signoff - hand (1). |
| | 3D | Invitational - hand (2). |
| | 2C | To be followed by 3D; forcing to game - hand (3). |

How does the opener rebid after responder's two clubs?

| Opener | Responder | |
|---|---|---|
| 1C | 1D | |
| 1NT | 2C | |
| 2H/2S | | Four card major. |
| 2D | | No four card major. |

| Opener | Responder | |
|---|---|---|
| 1C/1D | 1H | |
| 1NT | 2C | |
| 2S | | Four spades and perhaps three hearts. |
| 2H | | Three hearts but not four spades. |
| 2D | | Neither three hearts nor four spades. |

| Opener | Responder |
|--------|-----------|
| 1C/1D | 1S |
| 1NT | 2C |
| 2H | Four hearts and perhaps three spades. |
| 2S | Three spades but not four hearts. |
| 2D | Neither three spades nor four hearts. |

| Opener | Responder |
|--------|-----------|
| 1H | 1S |
| 1NT | 2C |
| 2S | Three card spade support, and perhaps five hearts. |
| 2H | Five hearts but not three spades.* |
| 2D | Neither five hearts nor three spades.* |

*Using five card majors, the two heart rebid shows five good hearts, and the two diamond rebid five bad ones, with a doubleton spade.

Notice that with this new method it is not the end of the world if opener occasionally bypasses a four card major. Responder can still check back by bidding two clubs if he is strong enough (upwards of 10 points). If he is not that strong, he usually bids the major at his first opportunity (if the suit is strong enough) so that it does not get lost in the shuffle. For example, partner opens one club, and you hold:

```
(1)  S. AKJx        (2)  S. AKJx
     H. xx               H. xx
     D. J10xx            D. KJxx
     C. xxx              C. xxx
```

With the first hand, it is better to respond 1S, as the hand is not worth two bids - you might as well take your best shot with your first one. With the second hand, you can respond 1D; if partner happens to rebid 1NT, you can bid 2C to check back in case partner happens to have 4S. For example:

| Opener | Responder | Opener | Responder |
|--------|-----------|--------|-----------|
| S. Jxxx | S. KQxx | 1C | 1D/1H |
| H. AJx | H. KQxx | 1NT | 2C |
| D. K10x | D. Qxxx | 2S | 4S |
| C. A10x | C. x | Pass | |

The assumption is that if responder bids 2C after responding in a major, thereby discovers a hidden four card major in the opener's hand, and still retreats to no trump, he must have had a five card major of his own - otherwise why did he bother with the 2C rebid?

54

| Opener | Responder | Opener | Responder |
|--------|-----------|--------|-----------|
| S. Axxx | S. Qx | 1C | 1H |
| H. KQx | H. AJxxx | 1NT | 2C |
| D. Axx | D. KJ10x | 2S | 2NT |
| C. Jxx | C. xx | 3H | 4H |
| | | Pass | |

When responder rebids 2NT, he shows the equivalent of a raise to 2NT with a five card heart suit. His most likely shape is 5-4-2-2. With 5-3-3-2 (particularly with a doubleton honor), he might elect to play in NT regardless. Opener knows that responder must have five hearts (he doesn't have four spades, and he doesn't have a two suiter or club support), so he shows three card support, and responder gambles on game.

Give responder the king of spades instead of the queen, and he might well leap to 3NT over 2S. Opener may still correct to 4H, as he knows responder must have a five card heart suit. Furthermore, he knows that responder's side suit, if he has one, must be diamonds - it can't be spades or clubs. (With spades he raises, and with clubs he bids them over 2S.)

What does this sequence mean?

| Opener | Responder |
|--------|-----------|
| 1D | 1S |
| 1NT | 2C |
| 2D | 2S |

This can best be used to show an invitational-range hand with a weak six card spade suit and outside strength.

| Opener | Responder | Opener | Responder |
|--------|-----------|--------|-----------|
| S. Q | S. A10xxxx | 1C | 1S |
| H. K10x | H. Ax | 1NT | 2C |
| D. AJxx | D. xxx | 2D | 2S |
| C. K10xxx | C. Qx | Pass | |

Opener should avoid rebidding 1NT with a small singleton in partner's suit, but with a singleton honor and a notrumpish hand it is certainly permissible.

| Opener | Responder | Opener | Responder |
|--------|-----------|--------|-----------|
| S. KJx | S. xx | 1D | 1H |
| H. xx | H. AJ9xx | 1NT | 3C |
| D. AKJxx | D. x | Pass | |
| C. J10x | C. KQxxx | | |

Responder describes an invitational two suiter. Opener, with a minimum, gives up the ship.

| Opener | Responder | Opener | Responder |
|--------|-----------|--------|-----------|
| S. J9xx | S. xx | 1C | 1H |
| H. Ax | H. KQxxx | 1NT | 2C |
| D. KJx | D. Ax | 2S | 3C |
| C. KJxx | C. A10xx | 3NT | Pass |

Opener rebids 1NT because it looks right with his secondary cards (1S would not be incorrect). Responder makes a forcing-to-game raise in clubs by first rebidding 2C. Opener elects to play 3NT. If opener had three hearts, he would have been compelled to bid 3H over 3C.

Furthermore, if opener had one unstopped suit, he would have bid the suit he did have stopped over 3C, to warn partner of his weakness in the other suit.

| Opener | Responder | Opener | Responder |
|--------|-----------|--------|-----------|
| S. Jxx | S. xx | 1C | 1H |
| H. Ax | H. KQxxx | 1NT | 2C |
| D. KQx | D. Ax | 2D | 3C |
| C. Axxxx | C. KQxx | 3D | ? |

At this point, responder, who has described a forcing-to-game hand with hearts and club support, knows that opener is weak in spades - and that lets no trump out. The final contract will be 5C or 4H.

A question may be forming in your mind. How do you play a contract of 2C? The answer is that you don't. That's what you are giving up in order to use the two-club gadget bid.

| Opener | Responder | Opener | Responder |
|--------|-----------|--------|-----------|
| S. K10x | S. x | 1D | 1H |
| H. Qx | H. Axxxx | 1NT | Help! |
| D. AKxxx | D. xx | | |
| C. Jxx | C. Q10xxx | | |

Responder obviously cannot bid 2C and then 3C, as that shows a forcing-to-game two suiter. It is also impossible to jump to 3C over 1NT (that shows an invitational-strength two suiter). What to do? All things considered, the best bet is to rebid 2H and hope partner has three card support. If he has a doubleton heart with three clubs, that's life. You haven't missed a game; and if you can squeeze out 2H, no matter how much more comfortable a contract of 2C would have been you have lost nothing.

For something really creepy, look at this hand again:

```
S. x
H. Axxxx
D. xx
C. Q10xxx
```

We saw how bad it was when partner opened 1D and then rebid 1NT. Do you want to see something worse? Assume partner opens 1C and then rebids 1NT over your 1H response. Keep in mind what your various club rebids mean.

| Opener | Responder | |
|--------|-----------|---|
| 1C | 1H | |
| 1NT | 2C | Strong hand; no bearing on the club suit. |
| | 3C | Invitational club-heart hand. Usually 10-12 points. |
| | 4C | Gerber, or something even more exotic, which we will see later. |

If this ever comes up, there are two ways out: (1) Rebid the hearts and swear you will get me the next time you see me. (2) Jump to 3C and pray partner either passes or bids 3H. If he double-crosses you and rebids 3NT, take this out to 4C (nonforcing).

Some of this misery can be eliminated by raising clubs immediately with hands like these:

```
S. A9xx        S. Q10xx
H. xx          H. xx
D. xx          D. xxx
C. QJxxx       C. AJ10x
```

Assume partner opens 1C. At rubber bridge, it must be right to respond 2C directly. At matchpoints, perhaps bidding 1S works best, but in my opinion it is better to raise the clubs; if an opponent (or partner) bids at the two level, you can then mention your spades. The theory that weak responding hands should limit themselves as quickly as possible has much merit.

In the real world, the bidding almost never goes that way when the responder has such a weak distributional hand. The opponents, you see, are usually getting into the act. If they are nice enough to bid diamonds, your club problems are solved.

| South | West | North | East |
|-------|------|-------|------|
| -- | -- | 1C | 1D |
| 1H | 1S | 1NT | Pass |
| ? | | | |

As South, you hold your favorite hand:

S. x    H. Axxxx    D. xx    C. Q10xxx

This time you can bid 2C not forcing! Why? When the opponents overcall in diamonds, you can use 2D as your artificial forcing bid. (All other rebids retain the same meaning.)

If the opponents overcall in a major suit, it does not pay to use the cue-bid as your artificial force because the bidding gets too high too soon. After a major-suit overcall and a 1NT rebid by partner, 2C is still artificial; but a cue-bid of the opponents' major promises a singleton in that suit and is forcing to game.

South holds:    S. x    H. Axxxx    D. Kxx    C. KQJx

| South | West | North | East |
|-------|------|-------|------|
| --    | --   | 1C    | 1D   |
| 1H    | 1S   | 1NT   | Pass |
| 2S    |      |       |      |

You'll teach them to overcall against you!

If the opponents have the audacity to double your partner's 1NT rebid, 2C by responder is natural and nonforcing. A redouble is the strength-showing call.

| South | West | North | East |
|-------|------|-------|------|
| --    | --   | 1D    | Pass |
| 1S    | Pass | 1NT   | Dbl. |
| ?     |      |       |      |

South should redouble with:   S. KJxxx    H. Kxxx    D. xx    C. Ax
but bid 2C (nonforcing) with:   S. Kxxxx    H. x    D. xx    C. QJxxx

Consider these sequences:

| Opener | Responder | | Opener | Responder |
|--------|-----------|--|--------|-----------|
| 1C     | 1D        | | 1C     | 1D        |
| 1NT    | 2H        | | 1NT    | 3H        |

In both auctions, responder has reversed, but in neither case has he first bid 2C to create a forcing situation. In the first sequence, responder is showing 10-11 H.C.P., with five diamonds and four hearts. Perhaps,

S. xx    H. QJ10x    D. AKxxx    C. xx

In the second sequence, responder's jump reverse shows six-five distribution, 8-10 H.C.P. Perhaps,

S. x    H. KQxxx    D. A10xxxx    C. x.

In neither case is the last bid forcing; it is merely invitational. To force, responder must first bid 2C over 1NT and <u>then</u> bid hearts.

At this point, I expect most readers are thinking to themselves, "Well, I think I understand what he is driving at, but if he adds just one more rule or makes it any more complicated, I'm not going to bother with it."

Good! I don't want you to read any further. Please don't read any further. You already have enough to get you to the right contract 90% of the time, and that's a lot better than you could possibly have done with your old method.

But I have been saving something special for those who can't stand 90% accuracy, don't mind memorizing, and have noticed that none of the examples have been strong responding hands with 5-4-3-1, 4-4-4-1, 5-4-4-0 or 6-3-3-1 distribution.

For you, here is something extra to make your partner remember.

| Opener | Responder | Opener | Responder |
|---|---|---|---|
| S. Ax | S. KQxxx | 1C | 1S |
| H. J10x | H. x | 1NT | 2C |
| D. Kxx | D. Axxx | 2D | ? |
| C. AQxxx | C. Kxx | | |

The rule, to refresh your memory, is that any new-suit bid by the responder is forcing to game if preceded by a 2C bid. Therefore, any <u>jump</u> in a new suit has a special meaning. It shows a three-suited hand with a singleton in the jump suit. In the example above, responder bids 3H.

Opener knows immediately that even <u>he</u> does not want to play no trump opposite a singleton heart. He has options at this point. The weakest bid he can make is game in any suit. The strongest bid he can make is to re-cue the singleton, normally showing either the ace or three or four small cards, both perfect holdings for possible slam contracts. If opener bids four of a minor, that is a mild slam try.

The point is that the hand will not play in no trump. And if you play a hand like this in either 4S or 5C, you can be proud of yourself. If you can work your way into 6C, I hope you make it; but I don't like your chances with a diamond lead.

Unless you are a super-expert, just try to get to the right game after one of these singleton-showing sequences and you will be miles ahead in the long run.

Although these singleton-showing jumps are great fun, you have to be careful about jumping to the four-level in your singleton suit, because you bypass 3NT. A jump to the four-level when preceded by 2C will usually have 15-16 high card points. It suggests a slam.

| Opener | Responder | Opener | Responder |
|--------|-----------|--------|-----------|
| S. A10x | S. KQxx | 1C | 1H |
| H. QJx | H. AKxxx | 1NT | 2C |
| D. Axx | D. x | 2H | 4D |
| C. QJxx | C. K10x | ? | |

At this point, opener should want to be in slam. But he does not know in which suit to play, because responder might have 4-4-4-1 distribution.

Might I suggest a convention I used to play with Bob Hamman to cover hands where we thought we had a slam but did not know in which suit? The confused party leaps to 5NT, which says: "Partner, remember our agreement that in a confusing auction a jump to 5NT says 'pick the best slam'? Well, this is it!" For some reason or other, most of our slam auctions were always very confusing and ended with one or the other leaping to 5NT in desperation. It's a great bid.

If a jump in a new suit preceded by 2C shows a singleton, it stands to reason that a double jump shows a void.

| Opener | Responder | Opener | Responder |
|--------|-----------|--------|-----------|
| S. KJx | S. - | 1C | 1D |
| H. KQx | H. A10xx | 1NT | 2C |
| D. Axx | D. KJxxx | 2D | 4S |
| C. Qxxx | C. AJxx | 5C | Pass |

Responder's jump to 4S shows a spade <u>void</u> (a jump to 3S would show a single-ton). Opener has wasted strength in spades and signs off at 5C, a reasonable contract.

Even slammish 6-3-3-1 responding hands can be shown.

| Opener | Responder | Opener | Responder |
|--------|-----------|--------|-----------|
| S. Kx | S. AQ10xxx | 1D | 1S |
| H. Axx | H. Kxx | 1NT | 4C! |
| D. KQ10xx | D. Axx | 4NT | 5H |
| C. J10x | C. x | 6D or 6S | Pass |

After a 1NT rebid, responder's direct jump to four of a minor shows a singleton in that suit with a 6-3-3-1 hand, and 13-15 high card points.  If the
hands fit perfectly, opener will know it and bid a slam.  To use this idea,
one would have to give up Gerber in this sequence.

| Opener | Responder | Opener | Responder |
|--------|-----------|--------|-----------|
| S. Axx | S. Kxx | 1D | 1H |
| H. Qxx | H. AKJ10xx | 1NT | 4D |
| D. KQJx | D. x | 4H | Pass |
| C. Jxx | C. K10x | | |

Here, opener knows responder's singleton diamond is opposite wasted diamond
strength, and signs off at 4H.

Enough exotica.  Back to the real world.  How does responder handle 5-4-3-1
hands that are not strong enough to bid 2C but are too strong for a signoff?

| Opener | Responder | Opener | Responder |
|--------|-----------|--------|-----------|
| S. KQx | S. x | 1C | 1D |
| H. Kxx | H. AJxx | 1NT | 2H |
| D. Jxx | D. KQxxx | ? | |
| C. KJxx | C. 10xx | | |

If responder's five-card suit is lower-ranking than the four-carder, he can
reverse - invitational.  In this case, opener has a tough problem because
he is dead minimum.  In theory, he should rebid 3D, or perhaps pass, but in
practice he will probably rebid 2NT.  Responder can then, if he wishes, bid
3C (nonforcing) and paint a fairly accurate picture of his hand.  Opener
bids 3D, which responder passes.

The real problem arises when responder's suits are reversed:

| Opener | Responder | Opener | Responder |
|--------|-----------|--------|-----------|
| S. Kxx | S. x | 1C | 1H |
| H. xx | H. KQxxx | 1NT | ? |
| D. K10x | D. AJxx | | |
| C. AKxxx | C. 10xx | | |

This is really bad news.  A rebid of 2D shows a much weaker hand, and a 2C
rebid forces us to bid 2NT over 2S, which is not terrible but not too palat-
able either.  It is possible to sign off directly at 2H, but that looks cow-
ardly; and a jump to 3D, though invitational, is a little misleading with
this distribution (partner will assume 5-5).  Come to think of it, I really
didn't have to add this hand to the article, did I?

Perhaps the best solution, with bad spot cards and only 10 high card points,
is to bid a nonforcing 2D and hope partner prefers with 2H.  You can then bid

either 3H or 3C (invitational). With good spot cards, an invitational jump to 3D is probably best. With the hand shown, opener passes 2D, and you miss your better club partial. No major catastrophe.

Better to end this with a minor disaster than for you to think that nothing ever goes wrong with this method. But this method is much better than what they call "Standard American." That I can promise you in spades; no, in clubs - two clubs, to be precise.

### Summary

After a 1NT rebid by opener, responder must decide whether he wants to discourage game (sign off), invite game, or force to game.

A. If he wishes to sign off (6-9 points), he can:

1. Pass.

2. Rebid his original suit.

3. Return to opener's original suit (but not clubs).

4. Bid a lower-ranking second suit.

B. If he wishes to invite game (10-12 points) he can:

1. Raise to 2NT.

2. Jump rebid his original suit.

3. Give opener a jump preference to his first suit.

4. Bid a higher-ranking suit.

5. Jump in a new suit, showing 5-5 distribution.

6. Bid a new suit and, if partner bids again, support partner's original suit, showing a 5-4-3-1 hand in this range.

7. Bid 2C as a checkback, then raise opener's second suit to the three-level, bid 2NT, or rebid his original suit at the two-level.

C. If he wishes to force to game (13 or more points), he must:

1. Jump to 3NT.

2. Jump to game in his original suit.

3. Jump to game in opener's suit.

4. Jump to four of a minor to show a singleton, 6-3-3-1 distribution, and 13-15-H.C.P.

5. Bid 2C and then:

      a. Bid a new suit.

      b. Jump in a new suit (showing a singleton).

      c. Double-jump in a new suit (showing a void).

      d. Take opener back to his first suit.

      e. Jump in his original suit.

If the opponents intervene with a 1D overcall, a rebid of 2D by responder (after opener's 1NT rebid) takes the place of the 2C bid. The 2C bid now becomes natural.

If the opponents overcall in a major suit, a cue-bid of that major by responder (after opener's 1NT rebid) shows a singleton in that suit and is forcing to game. 2C retains its normal artificial meaning.

If the opponents double the 1NT rebid, a redouble shows a strong hand (upwards of 10 points), while 2C is natural.

The Michael's Cue Bid is a direct cue bid of the opponent's suit to show a two-suited hand.

### A Cue Bid in the Minors

A direct cue bid of a minor suit opening bid shows a major two suiter, either 5-5 or 5-4 distribution, lacking the strength of a takeout double. The most likely range for this cue bid is 7-10 H.C.P.

Typical hands that would overcall an opening bid of either 1C or 1D with
2C or 2D are:

```
            (1)  S. AJ876     (2)  S. AQ76
                 H. KJ876          H. QJ987
                 D. 5              D. Q42
                 C. 76             C. 6
```

With only 5-4 distribution the Michael's bidder must keep one eye on the vulnerability as he risks a serious penalty.

### Responses to a Michael's Cue Bid in the Minors

In general, responder bids the full value of his hand. A bid of 2H or 2S is the weakest response. Unless the Michael's Cue Bidder has an exceptional hand where he planned to cue bid and then raise with something like:

```
                 S. AK876
                 H. AQ765
                 D. 54
                 C. 2
```

he simply passes.

A jump to 3H or 3S is invitational, and a jump to game means exactly what it says - although it could be an advanced sacrifice to confuse the opposition.

A response of 2NT shows a no trump hand with 15-17 H.C.P. and is not forcing.

A response of 2D to 2C shows diamonds and no interest in either major.

A second cue bid in the opponent's suit is the strongest bid the responder can make and asks the Michael's bidder to bid his longer major. The responder may have three cards in both majors with a game going hand and naturally wishes to play in the longer trump suit.

## A Cue Bid in the Majors

A direct cue bid in the majors shows the other major and an unspecified minor suit. The distribution of the cue bidder's hand will be either 5-5 or 6-4 with the six card suit being the minor.

All of these hands would cue bid 2S after an opening bid of 1S:

| | | | | | | | |
|---|---|---|---|---|---|---|---|
| (1) | S. 5 | (2) | S. 5 | (3) | S. 54 | (4) | S. 54 |
| | H. AQ765 | | H. AQ765 | | H. KQ87 | | H. KQ87 |
| | D. KQ876 | | D. 54 | | D. 2 | | D. AQ9875 |
| | C. 54 | | C. KQ876 | | C. AQ9875 | | C. 2 |

The range of the 2S cue bid is slightly higher (10-13) because partner is forced to respond at a higher level.

## Responses to a Major Suit Cue Bid

A response of 2NT asks the cue bidder to name his minor suit.

A response in the other major is natural and not forcing.

A second cue bid in the opponent's suit is forcing to game.

A response of 3NT is natural.

A response in a minor suit is to play and expresses no interest in finding out about the cue bidder's second suit.

## Defense to Michael's

It is easiest to defend against a Michael's Cue Bid in the minors because you know which two suits the cue bidder has.

For example, if the bidding begins:

| South | West | North | East |
|---|---|---|---|
| 1C | 2C | ? | |

North would bid as follows:

2NT would be natural and not forcing showing 10-12 balanced points.

3NT would be natural.

2H and 2S would show STOPPERS in that suit with a club fit, urging partner to bid no trump if he has the other major stopped. These responses typically describe hands in the 10-13 point range and promise one more bid if game has not been reached.

Double shows a hand that is interested in penalties; it probably denies a good club fit as no cue bid was made.

A raise to 3C is natural and a raise to 4C is preemptive.

A response of 2D is not forcing. With a good diamond hand responder must either double and then bid diamonds or jump to 3D directly. Both actions create a forcing situation.

If the cue bid has been in a major suit:

| South | West | North | East |
|-------|------|-------|------|
| 1H    | 2H   | ?     |      |

A raise to 3H shows 9-11.

A raise to 4H would be preemptive.

Double and then bidding 3H would show an opening bid with three card support. Forcing.

Double and then bidding 4H would show an opening bid with four card support.

A response of 2NT would show 10-12 balanced points. Not forcing.

A response of 3NT would be natural and to play. Probably 13-15.

Responses of three of a minor are not forcing and show long suits.

A bid of 2S would be natural showing strong spades as the cue bidder might have four spades to the jack or queen. Not forcing.

TOP AND BOTTOM CUE BID

Top and Bottom Cue Bids are direct cue bids in the <u>major</u> <u>suits</u> to show the other major plus clubs. The point count range is generally 10-13.

For example, if the opening bid to the right is 1H, holding the following hands you would overcall 2H:

```
(1)  S. AK87        (2)  S. K7654
     H. 54               H. 4
     D. 2                D. K2
     C. QJ10876          C. A10987
```

Similarly, if the opening bid were 1S the following hands would overcall 2S:

```
(1)  S. 4           (2)  S. A4
     H. AJ98             H. 97654
     D. 54               D. 2
     C. AQJ985           C. AK654
```

The advantage of Top and Bottom Cue Bids over Michael's Cue Bids is that responder immediately knows the cue bidder's two suits and cannot be pre-empted by third hand.

### Responses to Top and Bottom Cue Bids

A response of 2NT asks for clarification. If the cue bidder has a five card major he must bid it. Otherwise he bids his six card minor. The distribution for the Top and Bottom Cue Bid will be either 5-5 or 6-4 with the six card suit being the minor.

A minimum response in one of the cue bidder's suits is not forcing and shows no game interest.

A jump response in one of the cue bidder's suits is invitational.

A response of.3NT is natural.

A response in diamonds, the suit the cue bidder does not have, shows long diamonds and is natural.

### Defense to Top and Bottom Cue Bids

| South | West | North | East |
|-------|------|-------|------|
| 1S    | 2S   | ?     |      |

In this position North has options:

a) A raise to 3S should show a good solid raise to 2S. Typically 9-11 support points.

b) A raise to 4S is preemptive.

c) With a strong hand the responder cue bids one of the cue bidder's suits. For example, if North held:

    S. AQ76
    H. A2
    D. KQ87
    C. 654

he should bid 3H to indicate a control in that suit with a spade fit.

d) Double would indicate a hand that would normally have redoubled if second hand had doubled. Perhaps a big penalty is in the offing.

e) A response of 3D is not forcing. With a strong hand in diamonds responder must double first and then bid diamonds.

This is a convention designed to deal with preemptive opening bids of two and three of a suit.

Assume the opening bid to your right is 2H.  Playing Weiss your bids have the following meanings:

2S and 3D are natural, showing the suit.

2NT shows a club suit.

3C is a takeout double.

Double shows a balanced no trump type hand with at least 16 H.C.P.

The basic idea behind this convention is to be able to penalize the pre-empting opponents if both defending hands are balanced.  For example, if partner doubles an opening Weak Two Bid you know he has a balanced hand.  If you too have a balanced hand it usually pays to defend.

Now assume the bidding has gone as follows:

| West | North | East | South |
|------|-------|------|-------|
| 2S | Pass | Pass | ? |

In the balancing seat your bids have the following meanings:

3C, 3D and 3H are all natural.

2NT is the takeout double.

Double still shows the balanced hand with a minimum of 15/16 H.C.P.

## Weiss Against Three Bids

Against an opening three bid defensive bids in both the direct and passout positions are assigned the same meaning.

For example:

| East | South |
|------|-------|
| 3D | ? |

3H, 3S and 3NT are all natural.

4C is a takeout double.

Double shows a balanced hand and at least the strength of an opening bid of 1NT.

Here again the main idea is to be able to penalize the preemptive bidder if both hands are balanced.  For example, if partner doubles an opening bid of

3H and you hold:    S.  Jxxx
                       H.  Jxx
                       D.  xx
                       C.  Qxxx

you don't have to worry that your partner has a singleton or void in hearts and that the opponents will have an easy time in their contract. Partner has a balanced hand, so you should pass the double. Playing "Standard", partner might have either a balanced hand with a doubleton heart or a powerful hand with a singleton or void in hearts and responder must guess what to do.

The majority of experts now use the negative double, particularly those who play five card major suit openings. Indeed it is very difficult to play five card major openings without using negative doubles!

First things first. What is a negative double? A negative double replaces the penalty double in many sequences and becomes a takeout for the unbid suits, particularly the unbid major or majors.

| North | East | South | West |
|-------|------|-------|------|
| 1C    | 1S   | Dbl.  |      |

Not using negative doubles, South's double is for penalties, showing strong spades. Playing negative doubles South's double is for takeout, promising at least four hearts!

Why doesn't South just bid 2H? First, a two level response in hearts guarantees a five card suit, and second, South may not be strong enough to go to the two level, but may not wish to be shut out completely. South might have a hand such as:

```
S. xx
H. Axxx
D. Axxx
C. xxx
```

Remember, playing five card majors there is a strong likelihood that North has four hearts and perhaps only three clubs.

It is just too easy to miss a heart contract after a spade overcall. For that reason many experts play negative doubles over overcalls of one and two spades.

How strong should one be to make a negative double? Keep in mind that I am sticking my neck out here because no two expert partnerships play negative doubles alike. I'm quite serious.

In theory, at least, a negative double is a limited bid which, if made over a one level overcall, promises 7-9 H.C.P. and at least four card support for any unbid major. After a two level overcall it promises about 8-10 H.C.P.

If the doubler has more, he must come out of the bushes on his next bid. But the doubler must remember that his partner is assuming he has a moderately weak hand until he hears otherwise.

71

If the negative doubler follows up his double by bidding a suit it is not forcing. He is saying in effect that he was not strong enough to bid the suit directly.

| North | East | South | West |
|-------|------|-------|------|
| 1C    | 1S   | Dbl.  | Pass |
| 2C    | Pass | 2H    |      |

South promised four hearts with the double, but now that South has bid the suit he must have at least five hearts. He was not strong enough to bid 2H directly over 1S, so he limited his hand with a negative double and then showed his five card suit. South might have:

```
S. xxxx
H. AQ10xx
D. J10x
C. x
```

The only way the negative doubler can force his partner to game is to make a cue bid at his first opportunity. A single raise promises 9-11, a jump raise 11-13, a 2NT rebid 10-12, and a jump in a new suit although rare is simply highly invitational.

| North | East | South | West |
|-------|------|-------|------|
| 1D    | 1S   | Dbl.  | Pass |
| 2C    | Pass | 2S    |      |

South still has the four hearts that he promised with his negative double but apparently has more than the 7-9 H.C.P. his partner is expecting. He might have:

```
S. xxx
H. AKxx
D. Jxx
C. KJx
```

South did not bid 2H directly over the 1S overcall because it would have promised a five card suit and partner might jump raise to 4H with only three card support.

Negative doubles can also be used over overcalls of 1D to show support for both majors.

| North | East | South | West |
|-------|------|-------|------|
| 1C    | 1D   | Dbl.  |      |

South might have any of these hands:

```
S. Jxxx       S. AJxxx      S. QJxx
H. AQxx       H. J10xx      H. Axxxx
D. Jxx        D. xxx        D. Jx
C. xx         C. x          C. xx
```

Partner will assume four card support for each unbid major and about 7-9 H.C.P. If South later bids a major, he would be showing a five card suit. If South later cue bids he would be showing both majors with a stronger hand.

Negative doubles are also made over two level overcalls.

| North | East | South | West |
|-------|------|-------|------|
| 1S    | 2C   | Dbl.  |      |

South should have a hand that is not strong enough to mention a suit at the two level but strong enough not to be shut out completely. Typically, South will have support for both unbid suits and about 7/8 to 10 H.C.P.

```
S. xx          S. x
H. AJxx        H. AQxx
D. Kxxxx       D. Q10xx
C. xx          C. xxxx
```

Again, if South follows up a negative double by bidding a suit he promises a five card suit. And, as ever, a cue bid promises a stronger hand. Opener can assume 11-13 H.C.P.

What if you really wish to double for penalties?

| North | East | South | West |
|-------|------|-------|------|
| 1S    | 2C   | ?     |      |

Assume South holds:

```
S. x
H. K10x
D. Q9xx
C. A1087x
```

This is a perfect penalty double of 2C. But playing negative doubles you must not double! When holding good trumps the best bet is usually to pass. Partner is supposed to make every effort to keep the bidding open if his right hand opponent passes. If North is short suited in clubs and has any kind of opening bid he will double 2C, and you can then leave in the double.

If you simply can't bear the thought of partner passing with a minimum if you pass, simply bid 2NT (10-12) or 3NT (13-15) directly and don't worry about penalties.

Now a word to the opening bidder when partner makes a negative double. You are to assume that your partner has 7-9 H.C.P. with at least four cards in any unbid major and you must bid the full value of your hand directly because the negative doubler will usually pass any non-jump bid you make.

Assume you are North and the bidding has proceeded:

| North | East | South | West |
|-------|------|-------|------|
| 1C    | 1H   | Dbl.  | Pass |
| ?     |      |       |      |

North holds each of the following hands:

| (1) S. AQxx | (2) S. AQxx | (3) S. AQxx |
|-------------|-------------|-------------|
| H. xx       | H. xx       | H. Ax       |
| D. Kxx      | D. Kx       | D. Kx       |
| C. KJxx     | C. AKxxx    | C. AKxxx    |

Before making your rebid, remember your partner's double has shown 7-9 H.C.P. and four spades.

With (1) - Simply bid 1S to show a minimum hand.

With (2) - Jump to 3S because you would have jumped to three if your partner had responded 1S.

With (3) - Jump to 4S as you would have if partner had responded 1S.

A jump to 2S in this sequence shows about 16 support points for spades.

Perhaps the most common sequence where the negative double comes into play is the one we have already discussed:

| North | East | South | West |
|-------|------|-------|------|
| 1C    | 1S   | Dbl.  | Pass |
| ?     |      |       |      |

What do you think North should rebid with each of the following hands?

| (1) S. AQx | (2) S. AQxx | (3) S. xxx | (4) S. Ax | (5) S. xxx |
|------------|-------------|------------|-----------|------------|
| H. xx      | H. xx       | H. AQxx    | H. AQxx   | H. Ax      |
| D. Kxx     | D. Qx       | D. xx      | D. xx     | D. Kx      |
| C. KJxxx   | C. AKJ10x   | C. AKxx    | C. KQxxx  | C. AKJ10xx |

## Solutions

(1)  1NT  Very similar to rebidding 1NT over a one level response: 12-15 with at least one spade stopper.

(2)  2NT  A jump to 2NT in this sequence shows 16-18 H.C.P. and a slightly unbalanced hand because the opening bid was not 1NT.

(3)  2H   Raising partner's hearts with a minimum opening.

(4)  3H   Inviting game. Just as you would if partner responded 1H.

(5)  3C   Showing extra values and inviting game.

Many pairs use negative doubles after overcalls at the three and four levels. Of course, the higher the level the more apt the opener is to pass the double, particularly with a balanced hand.

Playing negative doubles comes in quite handy when South holds something
like this:

```
S. xxx
H. AKxx
D. AJxx
C. xx
```

The bidding:

| North | East | South | West |
|-------|------|-------|------|
| 1C    | 3S   | ?     |      |

South is very happy to double, not to show spade strength, but rather to
show "cards", points if you will. A negative double of an overcall at the
three or four level announces near opening bid values without a long suit.
Partner can do as he sees fit. Of course, if you really have their suit you
must exercise patience and usually pass. For example, if you hold:

```
S. AK95
H. 54
D. 107654
C. 32
```

it is risky to double 3S as North is going to assume you have the other kind
of hand and is very apt to remove your double to something very unappetizing -
like 4H. Better to pass and hope partner reopens with a double.

It all amounts to not being able to have your cake and eat it too. Most of
the time when there is a three or four level enemy preempt you are more apt
to have a hand with points and no long suit than a hand with strong trumps.
Thus the reason for negative doubles at higher levels.

For the neophyte it is probably best to start using negative doubles only
over one and two spade overcalls to test the waters. If you feel you can
handle those, then take on the bigger babies.

# THE RESPONSIVE DOUBLE

This is a relatively new convention which has considerable merit. Its main use arises after a takeout double followed by support:

| West | North | East | South |
|------|-------|------|-------|
| 1S   | Dbl.  | 2S   | Dbl.  |

In the good old days South's double was for business and it meant he was loaded in spades - either four very good ones or, more likely, five. In practice this occurs very rarely and the double can be put to better use.

If North-South decide to use Responsive Doubles, a double by South in this position says, "Partner, I have some scattered strength but no long suit. Why don't you bid your longest suit, I will have support for it." In other words, South is making a return takeout double for North to bid!

How strong must South be to make a Responsive Double? As Responsive Doubles are usually made at the two or three level South's strength will vary with the level at which he is forcing his partner to bid.

If North can still show his suit at the two level, South need have only seven or so points to make a Responsive Double.

| West | North | East | South |
|------|-------|------|-------|
| 1C   | Dbl.  | 2C   | ?     |

If South holds:   S. Q104   H. A76   D. J1076   C. 654
he doubles, forcing North to bid his best suit. If South actually bids a suit it is usually a long suit or a good four card major since he would use the Responsive Double for all balanced or semi-balanced hands.

In the first sequence, where the opponents have opened spades and South's double forces North to the three level, South should have at least eight working points-on up to eleven.

The following three hands would be examples of responsive doubles:

| West | North | East | South |
|------|-------|------|-------|
| 1S   | Dbl.  | 2S   | Dbl.  |

(1)  S. 1097    (2)  S. 32    (3)  S. 7654
     H. K87        H. 876       H. AJ8
     D. A765      D. AJ76     D. K8
     C. J108      C. KJ87     C. J872

Should West pass, North is supposed to bid his longest suit, keeping in mind that his partner probably does not have four cards in the unbid major.

(If South actually has four hearts he should mention the suit at his next opportunity after the Responsive Double.)

Therefore, if North has doubled 1S with    S. J4
                                                   H. Q543
                                                 D. K42
                                                 C. AKJ4

he should rebid 3C and not 3H after a Responsive Double from South. If he has extra values he must make a strong bid over his partner's Responsive Double. He must either jump in a suit, which is strongly invitational to game, or cue bid the opponents' suit, which is forcing to game. (Forcing smiles don't count.) A simple bid by the original doubler is not forcing and the responsive doubler will usually pass.

The Responsive Double is a limited bid. With an extremely strong responding hand (upwards of 12 H.C.P.) make a cue bid instead of a Responsive Double, forcing to game.

| | West | North | East | South |
|---|---|---|---|---|
| | 1H | Dbl. | 2H | ? |

South holds:

| (1) | S. AJ87 | (2) | S. KQ4 | (3) | S. A5 | (4) | S. 65 |
|---|---|---|---|---|---|---|---|
| | H. 4 | | H. 54 | | H. K1076 | | H. AQ |
| | D. K8765 | | D. AJ87 | | D. Q543 | | D. KQ765 |
| | C. A87 | | C. K654 | | C. 654 | | C. J765 |

With the first two hands South cue bids 3H, forcing the partnership to game. With the third hand South bids 2NT. (A Responsive Double is not made with excessive strength in the opponents' suit.) With the fourth hand South says 3NT. Again South has too much strength for a Responsive Double and too much strength in hearts for either a Responsive Double or a cue bid.

DO NOT MAKE RESPONSIVE DOUBLES OR CUE BIDS IN RESPONSE TO A TAKEOUT DOUBLE WITH HANDS THAT ARE WELL SUITED TO NO TRUMP. BID NO TRUMP.

What about sequences like this?

| West | North | East | South | or | West | North | East | South |
|---|---|---|---|---|---|---|---|---|
| 1S | Dbl. | 3S | Dbl. | | 3H | Dbl. | 4H | Dbl. |

What would a double by South mean at these levels? Is North forced to bid or is the double 100% for penalties when partner must bid at the four level?

Expert opinion is that North need not remove the double at the four level or higher, indeed not with a balanced hand. With an unbalanced or freak hand

the doubler should bid his long suit. It is unlikely, in view of the opponents' strong bidding in one suit, that South has trump strength; more likely
he has general strength without four cards in the unbid major.

Consider the bidding on this deal and see if it makes any sense to you.
North-South vul.

Dealer East

```
                              North
                              S. K87
                              H. Q108
                              D. 654
                              C. KQ32
            West                                East
            S. 109                              S. 532
            H. 9763                             H. 54
            D. K107                             D. AQJ9872
            C. A1098                            C. 4
                              South
                              S. AQJ64
                              H. AKJ2
                              D. Void
                              C. J765
```

The bidding:

| East | South | West | North |
|------|-------|------|-------|
| 3D   | Dbl.  | 5D   | Dbl.  |
| Pass | 5S    | Pass | Pass  |
| Pass |       |      |       |

East has a normal preemptive opening and South's double is, of course, for
takeout. West takes advantage of the vulnerability by furthering the preempt BEFORE the opponents have found their fit. This is a typical expert
tactic, and if you haven't been bidding this way, you should. (It drives
the opponents mad.) What is North supposed to do over 5D? He can do no
more than double to show cards (strength) and hope partner finds the right
path.

Now South is forced to use his judgment. Does his diamond void mean that
his partner is loaded in diamonds? This is naive thinking. The opponents
have been bidding diamonds as if there is no tomorrow and certainly have a
massive fit. So why is North doubling? You've heard about the man without
a country; well, North is a man without a suit. South must judge whether
it is better to defend at the five level or pursue his own game. With any
balanced or semi-balanced hand he will usually elect to defend. With his
actual hand he elects to bid 5S, certain that his partner must have some
useful cards. South will not always be right, but then again, who is?

As it turns out, South is right this time.  5D doubled is down two and 5S makes on the nose.  (And it only took me two hours to construct this "common" example hand.)

For those who like to delve even further into the unknown, Responsive Doubles can be used after partner overcalls and responder supports opener's suit.

| West | North | East | South |
|------|-------|------|-------|
| 1C | 1H | 2C or *3C | Dbl. |

*Limit Raise.

In ancient times this was also considered a penalty double.  But how often does bidding like this actually happen?  Right.  Not too often.  Using the double in this sequence (when opener's bid has been raised) as responsive to show support for the two unbid suits has great merit.  The overcaller now avoids rebidding his suit unless it is very long or strong and strives instead to support one of partner's suits.  Let's look at a few hands that might make a Responsive Double after the above sequence:

| | | | | | |
|---|---|---|---|---|---|
| (1) | S. AJ932 | (2) | S. AK87 | (3) | S. AJ87 |
| | H. 32 | | H. 4 | | H. A73 |
| | D. KQ983 | | D. KJ1098 | | D. K106 |
| | C. 3 | | C. 763 | | C. 543 |

The first two hands more or less conform to what partner expects -- nine or ten cards in the two unbid suits and sufficient strength to play somewhere at the three level.

The third hand requires explanation.  If you and your partner play that a jump raise to the three level over a one level overcall shows an opening bid in high card strength, you need not use the double followed by support to show this type of hand.  But if you play your jump responses to overcalls much the same as your jump responses to an opening bid (assuming you play limit raises, of course) you are going to find that you will have trouble responding to an overcall with a good hand.

The Responsive Double followed by support is the answer.  It does mean, however, that your double in this sequence can show one of two types of hands, and for that reason many players use the Responsive Double to show either the other two suits or support for the original suit, but not both.

You must decide whether you and your partner (particularly your partner) can handle such goings on.

In any event, if you decide to use the double in this sequence for takeout you should have a reasonably good hand approximating an opening bid; particularly if you tend to overcall light.

I suggest that, at first, you simply try the bid after a takeout double and a raise. If you find you can handle that you might try using it after an overcall and a raise to show the other suits, or support, or both. BUT AGREE BEFOREHAND. And remember, a Responsive Double can be used only if the opponents have bid and raised one suit.

The Flannery Two Diamond opening bid is used to handle a particularly awkward hand, one that has specifically five hearts, four spades and typically 12-15 H.C.P.

If hands like this are opened 1H it is impossible to mention the spades without reversing (which shows a bigger hand). Conversely, if the hand is opened 1S and hearts rebid, responder is misled about the major suit distribution of the opener's hand.

The Flannery convention solves the problem by using the 2D opening to show hands of this nature:

| (1) | S. AK76 | (2) | S. A987 | (3) | S. KQ104 |
|---|---|---|---|---|---|
| | H. KQ987 | | H. AK876 | | H. AJ876 |
| | D. J4 | | D. K54 | | D. Void |
| | C. 64 | | C. 8 | | C. K765 |

## Responding to Flannery

Here is a schedule of responses to 2D and their meanings:

2H,2S   Not forcing. Responder simply wants to play in that suit.

3H,3S   Not forcing; invitational. If opener is maximum he proceeds to game.

3C,3D   Not forcing; invitational. Responder should have a reasonable six card suit in the 11-13 range.

3NT   Mild slam try showing a balanced type hand with approximately 16-18 H.C.P.

4C   This can usefully be used as Gerber, by agreement, asking for aces.

2NT   This response is forcing to game by a non-passed hand and asks opener for more distributional information. Opener rebids as follows:

  3C   Shows three clubs and of necessity a singleton diamond.

  3D   Shows three diamonds and of necessity a singleton club.

  3H   Shows 4-5-2-2 and a minimum hand in high cards. Typically 12 or 13 H.C.P. (It is possible to open Flannery with as little as 11 H.C.P. but the distribution must be either 4-5-1-3, 4-5-3-1, 4-5-4-0 or 4-5-0-4.)

  3NT   Also shows 4-5-2-2 distribution but 14-15 H.C.P.

  3S   This can be used to show a hand with four spades and six hearts, a hand where opener simply cannot resist using his toy. Something like: S. AKJ8 H. J108765 D. K4 C. 2. If you do this you should have bad hearts and good spades.

  4C,4D   These show four card suits so of necessity a void in the other minor. These rebids are somewhat risky as they bypass 3NT.

A modification of the Flannery Two Diamond opening, also gaining in popularity, is to play the bid in a more natural sense. Open the bidding with 2H instead of 2D to show the 4-5 distribution in the majors. All responses are the same and the bid is easier to remember because you are bidding hearts when you actually have them.

If you play Flannery Two Diamonds you can still have your Weak Two Bid in hearts, but you cannot play Roman Two Diamonds to show a strong 4-4-4-1 hand. If you play Flannery Two Hearts you give up your Weak Two in hearts, but you can have your Roman Two Diamonds or a Weak Two in diamonds if you prefer.

In tournament bridge it is certainly better to play Flannery Two Diamonds and not give up your Weak Two in hearts. However, in rubber bridge or I.M.P. scoring it is probably better to play Flannery Two Hearts, particularly if you are familiar with Roman Two Diamonds.

### Examples of Flannery 2D (or 2H)

(1)

| Opener | Responder |
|--------|-----------|
| S. AQxx | S. Kxx |
| H. AKxxx | H. x |
| D. xx | D. Axxxx |
| C. xx | C. 10xxx |
| 2D or 2H | 2S |
| Pass | |

(2)

| Opener | Responder |
|--------|-----------|
| S. AQxx | S. KJx |
| H. QJxxx | H. xx |
| D. KQx | D. Jxx |
| C. x | C. AKJxx |
| 2D or 2H | 2NT |
| 3D (showing 3D and a singleton club) | 3NT |

(3)

| Opener | Responder |
|--------|-----------|
| S. Kxxx | S. Axxxxx |
| H. AKxxx | H. x |
| D. Kx | D. QJxx |
| C. xx | C. xx |
| 2D or 2H | 4S |
| Pass | |

(4)

| Opener | Responder |
|--------|-----------|
| S. KQxx | S. Ax |
| H. AQxxx | H. xx |
| D. x | D. KQ109xx |
| C. Kxx | C. Axx |
| 2D or 2H | 2NT |
| 3C | 3NT |

(5)

| Opener | Responder |
|--------|-----------|
| S. KJxx | S. Qx |
| H. AQ10xx | H. 9x |
| D. xx | D. KQxx |
| C. Kx | C. J10xxx |
| 2D or 2H | Convert 2D to 2H, Pass 2H. |

(6)

| Opener | Responder |
|--------|-----------|
| S. AQJx | S. Kxx |
| H. Qxxxxx | H. Kx |
| D. Ax | D. KJxx |
| C. x | C. Axxx |
| 2D or 2H | 2NT |
| 3S (6 hearts and 4 spades) | 4H |
| Pass | |

GERBER

"Gerber" is an ace-asking convention designed by John Gerber, Houston bridge expert. It replaces the Blackwood bid of 4NT with the ace-asking bid of 4C in certain specialized sequences.

Using the convention has certain advantages; aces can be asked for at a lower level and 4NT is available in its natural sense.

The problem with this convention is that partner sometimes thinks your 4C bid means clubs when it is asking for aces, and sometimes answers for aces when your 4C bid means clubs! In order to reduce the confusion and get the most out of this useful convention follow these simple guidelines.

1. Any jump to 4C over an opening bid of 1NT or 2NT is Gerber.

| Opener | Responder | | Opener | Responder |
|--------|-----------|--|--------|-----------|
| 1NT | 4C | | 2NT | 4C |

In both cases responder is asking for aces. Responses to 4C, Gerber are:

| | |
|--|--|
| 4D | zero or all four aces |
| 4H | one ace |
| 4S | two aces |
| 4NT | three aces |

If the 4C bid is followed by 5C partner is asking for kings. Responses are:

| | |
|--|--|
| 5D | zero kings |
| 5H | one king |
| 5S | two kings |
| 5NT | three kings |
| 6C | four kings |

If the 4C bidder rebids 4NT partner must pass!

2. A response of 2C, Stayman, followed by 4C is Gerber.

| Opener | Responder | |
|--------|-----------|--|
| 1NT | 2C | Responder inquires about a major suit and |
| 2H | 4C | then asks for aces. |

The same applies after an opening bid of 2NT.

| Opener | Responder | |
|--------|-----------|--|
| 2NT | 3C | Responder asks for a major and then asks |
| 3D | 4C | for aces. |

The corollary to this is: if responder first bids Stayman and then rebids 4NT, the 4NT is not Blackwood, it is natural.

3.  Any jump to 4C over 1NT or 2NT is Gerber.

| Opener | Responder | Opener | Responder | Opener | Responder |
|--------|-----------|--------|-----------|--------|-----------|
| 1D     | 2NT       | 1C     | 1H        | 1H     | 1S        |
| 4C     |           | 1NT    | 4C        | 2NT    | 4C        |

The last bid in each sequence is Gerber, asking for aces.

Now look at this somewhat similar sequence:

| Opener | Responder |
|--------|-----------|
| 1S     | 2C        |
| 2H     | 4C        |

Not Gerber because the 4C bid did not follow 1NT or 2NT.

The following advice must be added but I would not expect too many players to heed it.  However, I must set my conscience at ease.

You might not have noticed, but using our methods it is impossible to show a club suit once your partner has opened 2NT!

| Opener | Responder | Meaning |
|--------|-----------|---------|
| 2NT    | 3C        | Stayman |

| Opener | Responder |          |
|--------|-----------|----------|
| 2NT    | 3C        | Stayman  |
| 3H     | 4C        | Gerber   |

| Opener | Responder |        |
|--------|-----------|--------|
| 2NT    | 4C        | Gerber |

You see, there is no way the responder can show a club suit using the above methods.  But there is a way.

After a 2NT opening bid a jump to 4C should be clubs!  If responder wishes to ask for aces he can simply bid 3C first, and then 4C.

Another problem with the Gerber convention is after a bid of 3NT.  It is simple enough to jump to 4C over 1NT and 2NT to ask for aces but over 3NT there are other problems.

| Opener | Responder | Responder holds: | S. 43 |
|--------|-----------|------------------|-------|
|        |           |                  | H. 4  |
| 1S     | 2D        |                  | D. AK876 |
| 3NT    | ?         |                  | C. KQ1054 |

Responder wants to bid 4C to show clubs and he should be able to.

A reasonable way to play after a bid of 3NT is this:

A bid of 4C shows clubs.

A bid of 4NT is a raise in no trump.  Not Blackwood.

A jump to 5C is Gerber!   And the follow up is 6C for kings.

There, I've said it!

This is a convention especially designed for those players who feel inwardly compelled to open the bidding in the third or fourth seat with sub-minimum hands, hands that total only ten or eleven points.

In order for poor partner to know that the opening bidder does not have a bona fide opening, the late Douglas Drury of Canada devised the following convention:

| South | West | North | East |
|-------|------|-------|------|
| Pass  | Pass | 1H or 1S | Pass |
| 2C    |      |       |      |

South's 2C response asks North whether or not he is kidding.  If North is kidding he rebids 2D.  If North is not kidding and has a normal opening bid he bids something other than 2D, and the bidding proceeds normally from there.  (However, if the opener really has diamonds and a sound opening he does bid 2D, but does not pass when partner signs off at two of opener's original major.)

The Drury convention can only be used by a passed hand after partner has opened with a major suit.

| South | North | | South | West | North | East |
|-------|-------|-|-------|------|-------|------|
| S. AJ4 | S. KQ1032 | | Pass | Pass | 1S | Pass |
| H. 32 | H. Q98 | | 2C | Pass | 2D | Pass |
| D. K10873 | D. Q4 | | 2S | Pass | Pass | Pass |
| C. Q105 | C. J76 | | | | | |

South finds out North is kidding and signs off at 2S.  Had North a full opening bid he could rebid his spades, show a four card heart suit, rebid 2NT, or make a jump bid.

If you and your partner do not believe in opening super light hands in the third or fourth seat you can live beautifully without this convention.

Drury himself invented the convention in self defense.  He used to play regularly with Eric Murray, one of the world's great players.  Murray absolutely adored (he still does) opening light in third or fourth seat.  Drury always seemed to have a pretty good hand and never knew whether or not Murray was up to his old tricks.

He said that in the first five years of his partnership the bidding would often proceed:

| | South (Drury) | West | North (Murray) | East |
|---|---|---|---|---|
| | Pass | Pass | 1S | Pass |
| | 3S | Pass | Pass | Dbl. |
| | Pass | Pass | Pass | |

It always turned out that Murray was kidding and the opponents would pick up 800 points. After the invention of his new convention, Drury would respond 2C instead of 3S. Murray would inevitably rebid 2D and Drury would sign off at 2S. The opponents would still double, but now they would only get 500.

## REVERSE DRURY

In this very popular variation the opener rebids 2D to show an opening bid, rebidding his original major to deny an opening bid. Also, after a 1S opening bid and a 2C Drury response, a rebid of 2H by the opener also shows a full opening bid.

In both variations, the following chart applies:

| Opener | Responder (Passed Hand) | Meaning of rebid |
|---|---|---|
| 1♠ | 2♣ | |
| 2NT | | 15-17 balanced |
| 3C, 3D, 3H | | Strong two-suiter |
| 3NT | | 18-19 balanced |
| 4C, 4D, 4H | | Singleton (slam try) |

After a 1H opening bid and a 2C Drury, a rebid of 3♠ by the opener shows shortness.

After opener rebids at the two level, a 3C or 3D rebid by the responder shows a six card suit along with three card major suit support.

Any jump bid by the responder following a 2C response shows shortness.

# THE LIGHTNER SLAM DOUBLE

This convention designed by Theodore Lightner enables the partner of the opening leader to make a lead directing double of a slam contract.

A. <u>If the Doubler has Bid a Suit</u>:

1. Partner is forbidden to lead that suit.

2. Partner is forbidden to lead a trump.

3. Partner should assume that the double was either based upon a void suit or an unexpected AK (or AQ) in a suit bid by the opponents. (Very often dummy's first bid suit.)

B. <u>If the Doubler has not Bid a Suit</u>:

1. Partner is forbidden to lead the one unbid suit. (If there is only one.)

2. Partner is forbidden to lead a trump.

3. Partner should assume that the doubler has either a void or an unexpected AK (or AQ) in dummy's first bid suit or perhaps declarer's side suit.

| North | East | South | West |
|-------|------|-------|------|
| 1S | Pass | 3S | Pass |
| 4D | Pass | 4S | Pass |
| 6S | Pass | Pass | Dbl. |

West's double would presumably call for a diamond lead, the most unusual.

C. <u>If Both the Doubler and the Doubler's Partner have Bid a Suit</u>:

1. Partner is forbidden to lead the suit bid by the doubler.

2. Partner is forbidden to lead his own suit.

3. Partner is forbidden to lead a trump.

4. The doubler probably (certainly) wants a lead in the unbid or the fourth suit.

D. <u>Doubles of No Trump Slams Ask For a Lead in Dummy's First Bid Suit</u>.

1.  Players who make a preemptive bid and then double a slam contract are usually doubling because of a void.

2.  Players who have bid strongly and then double a slam usually have their strength in a different suit and wish to direct the opening leader away from the suit that they have bid.

3.  When in doubt lead dummy's first bid suit, although the double of a suit slam is in no way a command to do so.

In certain situations one player would give just about anything to know what his partner had in a particular suit. Blackwood doesn't help and cue bidding doesn't always either.

For example:    Say you pick up:    S. AQ4
                                   H. AKQ654
                                   D. A10
                                   C. 84

and your partner opens 3S. What is your response? The problem revolves around determining what partner has in one suit - clubs.

Partner could have any of these hands:

```
(1)  S. KJ109765      (2)  S. KJ109765      (3)  S. KJ109543
     H. 32                 H. 32                 H. 32
     D. K76                D. K9                 D. 87
     C. 2                  C. J10                C. A2
```

Opposite (1) - 6S is a laydown.

Opposite (2) - six cannot be made because of the two club losers.

Opposite (3) - seven is a laydown.

Incidentally, responder has the same problem if the opening bid is 4S.

True enough, for (3) Blackwood solves the dilemma, but what about (1) and (2)?

The real solution is to play asking bids over preemptive openings with the following partnership agreement:

1. Any <u>jump</u> response to an opening bid of three is an asking bid in that suit.

   | Opener | Responder | |
   |--------|-----------|---|
   | 3S | 5C | What do you have in clubs? |

   | Opener | Responder | |
   |--------|-----------|---|
   | 3D | 4H | What do you have in hearts? |

2. Any new suit response at the five level to an opening bid of four of a major is an asking bid.

   | Opener | Responder | |
   |--------|-----------|---|
   | 4H | 5D | What do you have in diamonds? |

   | Opener | Responder | |
   |--------|-----------|---|
   | 4S | 5C | What do you have in clubs? |

None of this interferes with normal bidding procedures because a new suit in response to an opening three bid is forcing so responder need not jump to get to game. The jump can be used more profitably. Furthermore, when partner opens four of a major he is supposed to have a very powerful suit and responder will not have a better suit very often. He is much more apt to want to make an asking bid.

## Responses to Asking Bids

Let's take an example sequence:

| Opener | Responder | |
|--------|-----------|--|
| 3S | 5C | What do you have in clubs? |

Responses to asking bids always start with the next suit; in this case 5D is the first step.

First step = two or more quick losers  xx, xxx, xxxx

Second step = singleton

Nearest no trump regardless of which step = king

Fourth step = Ace

Fifth step  = Ace-King or Ace-Queen

Sixth step  = Void

Examples:

| Opener | Responder | | Opener | Responder |
|--------|-----------|--|--------|-----------|
| S. K4 | S. 87 | | 3D | 4S |
| H. 65 | H. AKQJ109 | | 4NT | 6NT |
| D. AJ109432 | D. K4 | | | |
| C. 43 | C. AKQ | | | |

Responder asks opener about spades. Opener shows the king and responder allows opener to play the hand at no trump to protect his king. Notice that in this case the first step is no trump, showing the king. With two or three small spades opener would respond 5C to the 4S asking bid.

| Opener | Responder | | Opener | Responder |
|--------|-----------|--|--------|-----------|
| S. AKJ98765 | S. Q104 | | 4S | 5H |
| H. 32 | H. J7 | | 5S | Pass |
| D. 2 | D. AKQJ | | | |
| C. 54 | C. AKJ10 | | | |

Responder asks about hearts and opener shows two or more quick losers in hearts. Responder signs off at 5S.

Asking bids can be used in certain other sequences that require partnership agreement. There is no disaster worse than a misunderstood asking bid!

A Fragment Bid is an unusual jump which shows primary (four or more cards) support for partner's last bid suit, a controlling card in the jump suit and a singleton in the unbid suit.

If the opener makes a Fragment Bid it is usually done by jumping one level higher than a jump shift or by making a jump reverse; e. g.,

| Opener | Responder |
|--------|-----------|
| 1C | 1S |
| 3H | |

| Opener | Responder | | Opener | Responder |
|--------|-----------|--|--------|-----------|
| S. AKxx | S. QJxxxx | | 1D | 1S |
| H. x | H. xxx | | 4C | 4NT |
| D. KQxxx | D. Ax | | 5H | 6S |
| C. AJx | C. xx | | Pass | |

Opener's unusual jump shows primary spade support (four or more cards), a control in clubs, and a singleton heart. Responder, assured of no more than one heart loser, can visualize a slam.

Responder can also make a Fragment Bid. The most useful sequences come after opener has rebid his original suit.

| Opener | Responder | | Opener | Responder |
|--------|-----------|--|--------|-----------|
| S. AKxxxx | S. QJx | | 1S | 2D |
| H. xxx | H. x | | 2S | 4C |
| D. Ax | D. KQJxx | | 4NT | 5D |
| C. xx | C. Axxx | | 6S | Pass |

Responder's jump promises a spade fit, first or second round club control and a singleton heart. It is a slam try. Opener realizes that he has one heart loser at most and can go to a slam. Had opener wasted values in hearts, say the king or the king-queen, he would sign off at 4S.

"Splinter Bids" are the same as Fragment Bids only the jump is in the single- ton suit rather than the three or four card side suit.

The above are the most common of the fragment sequences. Every partnership has other specialized sequences, but they must be talked over and memorized.

It is always dangerous to compete against a strong no trump simply because the partner of the no trump opening bidder is in such a good position to double your overcall, knowing partner has a strong balanced hand. Furthermore, game is unlikely anytime an opponent opens with a strong no trump so the main reason for competing is to fight for a partial and to indicate a lead if the responder plays the hand.

There are two "no-no's" to remember: (1) Do not overcall an opening 1NT bid with one five card suit. One should have at least a six card suit or a two suiter. (2) Do not overcall if you have a solid suit. Remember as of now the hand is still in no trump and you are on lead. If the opponents exit to a suit you can then mention your solid suit.

Keeping this all in mind I think the best convention yet devised to cope with a strong no trump opening is "Roth-Stone Astro." It goes like this:

After an opening bid of 1NT any overcall at the two level shows the suit bid plus SPADES. An overcall of 3C or 3D shows the suit bid plus HEARTS. With all reasonable one-suited hands (at least a six card suit)--DOUBLE. An overcall of 3H or 3S is preemptive very much like an opening three bid. An overcall of 2NT shows the minors.

Using this convention you can enter the auction with relative safety if you have a two suiter. A two suiter is generally defined as 5-5 or 6-4 with the four being the major and the six the minor. With six cards in the major it is better to double to show a one suiter.

In general, to make one of these overcalls you should have at least 10 points in high cards and most of them should be in your long suits. You should also keep an eye on the vulnerability if you are thinking of entering with an over-call at the three level. Furthermore, you should look at the intermediate spot cards in your two suits on borderline hands.

An overcall of 2H shows hearts and spades with longer hearts. An overcall of 2S shows hearts and spades with longer spades. With equal length, over-call 2H.

Keep in mind that this convention is not a toy but a useful gadget which allows you to enter the auction with a two suited hand.

Assume you hold the following hands with both sides vulnerable and your right hand opponent opens 1NT.  Playing Roth-Stone Astro, what call would you make?

| | | | | |
|---|---|---|---|---|
| 1. | S. A4 | H. K765 | D. Q9876 | C. Q5 |
| 2. | S. KQ876 | H. 5 | D. AQ876 | C. 76 |
| 3. | S. KJ104 | H. 5 | D. A2 | C. KQ9865 |
| 4. | S. 5 | H. K4 | D. KJ10876 | C. AQ54 |
| 5. | S. K4 | H. 3 | D. KJ876 | C. AJ1087 |
| 6. | S. QJ108764 | H. K654 | D. 2 | C. 5 |
| 7. | S. A76 | H. K54 | D. KQ8 | C. A654 |
| 8. | S. 4 | H. A8765 | D. KQ8765 | C. 2 |
| 9. | S. KQ87 | H. AJ1098 | D. A54 | C. 2 |
| 10. | S. AK432 | H. K5 | D. Q87 | C. J43 |

=== Solutions ===

1. Pass — This is not considered a two suiter.

2. 2D — Showing diamonds and spades.

3. 2C — Showing clubs and spades.

4. Double — Showing a one suiter.

5. 2NT — Showing a minor two suiter.  At least 5-5.

6. 3S — Preemptive.

7. Pass — You can no longer double a strong NT with a balanced hand and 16-18 points.  Your partner will think you have a one suiter.  If you are stronger you can double and then when your partner bids 2C to find out your suit, you can bid 2NT to show a 19-20 point balanced hand, but this will never happen in reality.

8. 3D — Showing diamonds and hearts.

9. 2H — Showing hearts and spades with better hearts. Only with a major two suiter should you have as few as nine cards in your two suits; otherwise, ten.

10. Pass — No more silly overcalls on five card suits.

## Responding to an Overcall

In general, when your partner overcalls, he simply is asking for a preference for one of his TWO SUITS.  Remember, he always has a two suiter.  With an equal number of cards in each of his suits, it is usually best to pass as he is apt to be longer in the suit he has bid.

With a strong responding hand you can either raise your partner's suit or jump prefer the other suit. To do this you should have a good working hand opposite a two suiter. That means that you should have aces, not kings and queens in partner's short suits, as well as some trump support and perhaps a fitting honor in his other suit.

If partner overcalls in a major (showing a major two suiter) go to the three level with 10-12 support points and bid game with more.

## When Partner Doubles

Partner's double shows an unspecified one suiter. Responder will normally make the artificial response of 2C to inquire about the suit. The doubler will then bid his suit and responder will usually pass.

If the responder is strong enough - usually 10 H.C.P. or more - he may elect to pass the double knowing that the doubler has a good suit to lead and a probable outside entry. If the responder bids any suit other than 2C in response to the double, he is saying that he does not want to hear the doubler's suit but wants to play it in his own suit. The responder would normally need a seven card suit to make such a bid as the doubler is marked with a six card suit of his own.

## Defense to Roth-Stone Astro

The best defense as the responder to the opening no trump bidder when an opponent doubles is to redouble with eight or more H.C.P. and bid naturally if you do not redouble. In other words, 2C is still Stayman and if you play Jacoby Transfer Bids they are still in effect. Otherwise, new suits at the two or three level are not forcing. Jumps are forcing.

If an opponent overcalls to show a two suiter a double is for penalties, a new suit is not forcing, and a cue bid in the opponent's suit is Stayman.

OTHER DEFENSIVE CONVENTIONS OVER OPPONENT'S ONE NO TRUMP OPENING

There are a number of other simpler conventions that can be used to cope with an opening 1NT.  Here they are in their simplest form.**

I. LANDY
- Overcall 2C to show a major two suiter.  All other overcalls are natural.  Double is for penalties.

### Responses to Landy

2D, 2H, 2S    To play.

2NT           Forcing and asking the 2C bidder to bid his longer major.  Responder probably has three of each major and wants to play in the longer suit.

3C            Forcing to game.  Evidently responder has a magnificent hand.

3D            Invitational jump in diamonds.

3H, 3S        Invitational.  Not forcing.

3NT           He wants to play it there.

4H, 4S        Responder thinks he can make game.

II. MY MODIFICATION OF LANDY
- Overcall 2C to show a major two suiter, overcall 2D to show a red two suiter.  All other overcalls are natural.  Double is for penalties.

III. BECKER
- Overcall 2C to show a minor two suiter, overcall 2D to show a major two suiter.  Double is for penalties.  All other overcalls are natural.

IV. RIPSTRA
- Overcall 2C to show a major two suiter with length in clubs.  Overcall 2D to show a major two suiter with length in diamonds.  The best hands to use this convention with are 4-4-4-1 or 5-4-3-1.  Double is for penalties.  All other overcalls are natural and show a one suiter.

V. ASTRO
- Overcall 2C to show hearts and a lower ranking suit.  Overcall 2D to show spades and a lower ranking suit.  A response of 2NT is forcing and asks for further information.

VI. PIN POINT ASTRO OR BROZEL
- 2C shows clubs and hearts.
2D shows diamonds and hearts.
2H shows hearts and spades.
2S shows spades plus an unspecified minor.  (Responder must bid 2NT to find out which minor.)
2NT is for the minors.
Dbl. shows a one suiter.  (Responder bids 2C to find out which suit.)

**Note: All of these conventions, including Roth-Stone Astro, are used in either the direct position (directly after the no trump opener) or in the fourth position if the no trump opening bid has been followed by two passes.

Many slam hands revolve around the trump suit, particularly those hands you
are considering bidding to a <u>grand</u> slam. Unless there are ten trumps between yours and partner's hands, including the ace and king, you should not
bid a grand slam without the top <u>three</u> honors. The GRAND SLAM FORCE is a
convention used to determine if you have these honors.

In caveman days the convention went something like this: after a suit had
been agreed upon, a leap to five no trump by either player asked about
honors in the trump suit. The player being asked leapt to seven of the
agreed suit if he had two of the top three honors, and signed off at six
if he did not. This variation would work for about 40% of the hands - not
quite enough, is it? A much more useful version of the Grand Slam Force
is presented below.

For openers, and don't let this scare you, there are two sets of responses.
If you have shown a strong suit by your previous bidding, your responses
will differ from those used when your bidding has not indicated a strong
suit. The definition of a strong suit is any of the following:

    1. A preemptive opening bid or overcall.

    2. A jump rebid.

    3. A rebid in your original suit after partner has made a jump shift.

I.   If you have shown a strong suit in your previous bidding and your part-
    ner leaps to five no trump,

| Opener | Responder |
|--------|-----------|
| 3S | 5NT |

Your responses are as follows:

| | |
|---|---|
| 6C | One of the top three honors, almost always the ace or king. |
| 6 of the agreed suit | Two of the top three honors. |
| 7 of the agreed suit | The top three honors. |

| Opener | Responder | Opener | Responder |
|--------|-----------|--------|-----------|
| S. AQJxxxxx | S. x | 4S | 5NT |
| H. x | H. AKQxx | 6S | Pass |
| D. xx | D. AKxx | | |
| C. Kx | C. AJx | | |

Responder inquires about opener's spades, the only possible problem.

Opener shows two of the top three honors and responder settles for six, knowing a high honor in spades is missing. Had opener the three top spade honors he would leap to seven spades.

| Opener | Responder | Opener | Responder |
|--------|-----------|--------|-----------|
| S. xx | S. AKxxxx | 3H | 5NT |
| H. AJ10xxxx | H. Qx | 6C | 6H |
| D. Kxx | D. A | Pass | |
| C. xx | C. AKxx | | |

Responder, looking for a grand slam if opener has two of the top three heart honors, leaps to five no trump, the Grand Slam Force. Opener shows one of the top three by responding six clubs and responder settles for a small slam.

| Opener | Responder | Opener | Responder |
|--------|-----------|--------|-----------|
| S. AKQxx | S. Jxx | 1S | 3H |
| H. xx | H. AKQxx | 3S | 5NT |
| D. KJx | D. None | 7S | Pass |
| C. xxx | C. AKQxx | | |

Opener shows the top three honors by leaping to seven. Had opener only two of the top three honors he would respond six spades, which the responder would pass.

Notice that when a suit has not actually been agreed upon, the last bid suit is the one that the five no trump bidder is interested in.

| Opener | Responder | Opener | Responder |
|--------|-----------|--------|-----------|
| S. AJ10xxxx | S. Kx | 1S | 2D |
| H. x | H. AKJxx | 3S | 5NT |
| D. Kx | D. A10xxxx | 6C | 6S |
| C. AKx | C. None | Pass | |

Responder smells an easy grand slam if opener has both the ace and queen of spades. Opener announces possession of only one of the top three honors and responder settles for six spades. Substitute the queen of spades for the jack and a grand slam would be a laydown.

II. If your previous bidding has not guaranteed a strong suit these are the responses:

6C  The queen or less.

6D  The ace or king with minimum length for your previous bidding.

6H  The ace or king with maximum length for your previous bidding.

6S  Two of the top three honors.

7C  The top three honors.

Because the response of six clubs might or might not show the queen, the five no trump bidder can inquire about the queen by bidding six diamonds over six clubs (if diamonds is not the agreed suit). With no queen, responder signs off at six of the agreed major. With the queen, responder bids seven as asked.

The jump to seven clubs to show the top three honors is optional. You could also jump to seven of the agreed suit. But there is a reason for jumping to only seven clubs. The five no trump bidder might want to play the hand in seven of his suit after discovering you have the top three honors in your suit. If your response by-passes his suit that option is no longer available.

Here's one that happened to me long ago and I have never forgotten it.

| Opener | Responder | | Opener | Responder |
|--------|-----------|---|--------|-----------|
| S. J10xxx | S. KQxxx | | 1S | 7S |
| H. AKx | H. None | | Pass | |
| D. x | D. AKJ10xxxx | | | |
| C. AQxx | C. None | | | |

As you can see my 'long ago' bidding was not very successful. Even my partner, a wonderful player, could not make this hand. Today I could get to the right contract in no time.

| Opener | Responder |
|--------|-----------|
| 1S | 5NT |
| 6C | 6S |
| Pass | |

I would ask my partner about his spade holding. He would show me the queen or less and I would give up on the grand slam.

| Opener | Responder | | Opener | Responder |
|--------|-----------|---|--------|-----------|
| S. Axxxxx | S. Kxxx | | 1S | 5NT |
| H. xx | H. AKJxxx | | 6H | 7S |
| D. QJx | D. AKx | | Pass | |
| C. Ax | C. None | | | |

Responder asks about opener's spades and opener shows either the ace or king with maximum length for his previous bidding. This usually means a six card suit. With four or five spades, opener would bid six diamonds.

Now the responder, knowing that there are ten trumps between the two hands, can safely contract for a grand slam, relying on the strong percentage that one player will not hold all three missing trumps.

99

Notice that in all of the examples given the five no trump bidder did not precede the bid with four no trump. Five no trump after four no trump asks for kings, of course. Is it possible to use the Grand Slam Force after checking for aces? Yes.

If the four no trump bidder follows up his request for aces with six clubs (assuming this is not the agreed suit), that becomes the Grand Slam Force. Responses are as follows:

I.   If your previous bidding has shown a strong suit:

6D                                      One of the top three honors.

6H, 6S                                  Two of the top three honors.

7C (or seven of the agreed suit)    The three top honors.

II.  If your previous bidding has not promised a strong suit:

6D                                      The queen or less.

6H, 6S                                  The ace or king.

7C (or seven of the agreed suit)    Two of the top three.

| Opener | Responder | Opener | Responder |
|--------|-----------|--------|-----------|
| S. KQJ10xxxx | S. A | 4S | 4NT |
| H. x | H. AKQxx | 5D | 6C |
| D. x | D. AKxx | 6S | 7S or 7NT |
| C. Axx | C. KQx | | |

Responder first must find out about aces. Once relieved that he and his partner hold all four aces, the responder makes the Grand Slam Force request of six clubs. Opener, who has previously shown a strong suit, responds six spades to show two of the top three. Responder confidently bids the grand slam. Change opener's spades to KJ10xxxxx and his response to six clubs would be six diamonds. Responder would then sign off at six spades, knowing one of the top spade honors was missing.

When playing Weak Two Bids the 2C opening is used for all game going hands. It is a completely artificial opening bid and the opener clarifies the nature of his hand on the rebid.

If the opening bidder has a long suit he rebids the suit and if he has a strong balanced hand he rebids either 2NT or 3NT. When playing Weak Twos the opening 2NT has a new range of 20-22 (22 only with 4-3-3-3 distribution or another flaw such as no aces or a KQ or QJ doubleton combination).

The opening bid of 2C followed by a rebid of 2NT describes a balanced hand in the 22-24 range. An opening bid of 3NT shows 25-26 and an opening bid of 2C followed by a jump rebid to 3NT shows a balanced 27-28.

Before going any further with the 2C opening it is necessary to discuss the responses. Currently there are three methods used to respond to an opening 2C bid. You and your partner should pick the one you like best.

### Methods of Responding to a 2C Opening

I. Two Diamonds Automatic

Using this method the responder automatically responds 2D allowing the opener to describe his hand at the lowest level possible. The responder may bid a suit but the suit must contain at least two of the top three honors, typically five or more cards.

The advantage of this method is that the opening bidder can either rebid his suit or no trump without having to increase the level; the disadvantage is that the opener has no idea whatsoever of the responder's strength.

When using this method the responder must clarify the strength of his hand on the rebid. This is very simple if the opener rebids 2NT or 3NT as the responder assumes captaincy and can pass, use Stayman, Gerber or Jacoby if you use these conventions.

Problems arise when the opener rebids a suit.  Most experts either
use a double negative or a second negative after opener rebids a
major suit on this common sequence:

| Opener | Responder |
|--------|-----------|
| 2C | 2D (automatic) |
| 2H or 2S | ? |

Now there are three ways to handle this:  (1) is to play 3C as the
second negative to show that the 2D bidder really was busted and, of
course, the 3C bid has nothing to do with clubs or (2) use 2NT as the
second negative freeing 3C to be a natural rebid or (3) use both 2NT
and 3C as second negatives.  2NT shows a weak hand in the 4-6 range
and 3C shows an even weaker hand in the 0-3 range.  When playing
second negatives the opener must realize that if the responder does
not use a second negative he must have a fairly good hand.

This might be the best way to handle responses to a 2C opening but
the feeling here is that you had best be an expert to play these responses.  Besides there are further complications with this method
if the opener rebids three of a minor over the semi-automatic 2D response.

Examples of this method:

| Opener | Responder |   | Opener | Responder |
|--------|-----------|---|--------|-----------|
| S. AKJxxx | S. xx |   | 2C | 2D |
| H. AKxx | H. Qxxx |   | 2S | 2NT or 3C (depending upon |
| D. Ax | D. xxx |   |    | your methods) |
| C. x | C. xxxx |   | 3H | 4H |
|        |           |   | Pass | |

| Opener | Responder |   | Opener | Responder |
|--------|-----------|---|--------|-----------|
| S. AKx | S. xxxx |   | 2C | 2D |
| H. KQx | H. xx |   | 2NT | Pass |
| D. AKxx | D. Jxxx |   |    | |
| C. KJx | C. 10xx |   |    | |

As most experts play, the only time the responder can drop the bidding
short of game after a 2C opening is if the rebid is 2NT and then the
responder must have less than three points.

| Opener | Responder | | Opener | Responder |
|--------|-----------|--|--------|-----------|
| S. Ax | S. xxx | | 2C | 2D |
| H. KQJxxx | H. Axxx | | 2H | 3H |
| D. AKQx | D. xx | | 3S | 4C |
| C. x | C. Axxx | | 4D | 4H |
| | | | 4NT | 5H |
| | | | 5NT | 6C |
| | | | 6H | Pass |

A direct raise of opener's major is a positive response and stronger than a double raise as it gives the opener more room to cue bid if he wishes. A direct double raise denies any outside aces or kings. It could conceivably contain a high trump honor or a singleton but never both.

| Opener | Responder | | Opener | Responder |
|--------|-----------|--|--------|-----------|
| S. AJx | S. KQxxx | | 2C | 2S |
| H. AKxxx | H. xx | | 3S | 4C |
| D. AKQJ | D. xxx | | 4NT | 5D |
| C. x | C. Axx | | 5NT | 6D |
| | | | 7S | Pass |

Opener knows responder must have the king-queen of spades for his positive response. He can count thirteen tricks including a club ruff in dummy.

II. Control Showing Responses

Using this method the responder simply shows the number of controls (king = one control; ace = two controls) he has on the first response with absolutely no regard to distribution. The responses are:

| Opener | Responder | Meaning |
|--------|-----------|---------|
| 2C | 2D | One control or less. |
| | 2H | Two controls. Either one ace or two kings. |
| | 2S | Three controls. One ace and one king. |
| | 2NT | Three controls. Three kings. |
| | 3C | Four or more controls. |
| | 3D, 3H, 3S | These responses all show one loser suits. |
| | 4C, 4D, 4H, 4S | These responses all show solid suits. |

After the initial control showing responses all rebids by both opener and responder are natural. In effect this is very similar to many of the popular 1C forcing systems, the only difference being level. Instead of opening an artificial 1C bid and responder showing controls, opener begins with 2C and responder shows controls.

| Opener | Responder | Opener | Responder |
|--------|-----------|--------|-----------|
| S. AKx | S. Qxxx | 2C | 2D (One control or less) |
| H. AQx | H. Kxxx | 2NT | 3C (Stayman) |
| D. KQxx | D. xx | 3D | 3NT |
| C. AJx | C. xxx | Pass | |

| Opener | Responder | Opener | Responder |
|--------|-----------|--------|-----------|
| S. AQJxxx | S. Kx | 2C | 2NT (Three kings) |
| H. AQJ | H. Kx | 6NT | Pass |
| D. x | D. Kxxxxx | | |
| C. AKQ | C. xxx | | |

Opener can count twelve tricks knowing partner has three kings.

| Opener | Responder | Opener | Responder |
|--------|-----------|--------|-----------|
| S. QJ109xx | S. xx | 2C | 2S (One ace and one king) |
| H. AKQ | H. xxx | 3S | 4C |
| D. AKQx | D. xxx | 4S | Pass |
| C. --- | C. AKxxx | | |

Opener realizes that responder's ace-king is very likely to be in clubs so makes the discouraging rebid of 4S. If responder had, say, the ace of clubs and the king of spades he would probably make another move.

III. Natural Responses with Two Diamonds Negative

Using this method all responses are natural and 2D is the negative the equivalent of the 2NT response to a strong two bid. New suit responses generally show reasonable five or six card suits with at least 7 H.C.P. A response of 2NT is natural and generally shows 7-9 H.C.P. and a balanced hand. A response of 3NT shows 10-12 H.C.P. and a balanced hand. In order to show a positive response in diamonds the responder must leap to 3D. Jump responses to 3H or 3S promise one loser suit and all jumps to the four level promise solid suits.

| Opener | Responder | Opener | Responder |
|--------|-----------|--------|-----------|
| S. AQ | S. xx | 2C | 2D (Weak hand) |
| H. AKJx | H. xxx | 3C | 3D (Help!) |
| D. x | D. xxxxx | 3H | 4C |
| C. AKxxxx | C. J10x | 4S | 5C |
|  |  | Pass |  |

| Opener | Responder | Opener | Responder |
|--------|-----------|--------|-----------|
| S. AKxx | S. xx | 2C | 2H |
| H. KQx | H. A10xxx | 5NT (Grand | 6D (Ace or king |
| D. --- | D. Kxx | Slam | with minimum |
| C. AKQJxx | C. xxx | Force) | length) |
|  |  | 7C | Pass |

See pages 97-100 on the Grand Slam Force to better understand this sequence. If responder did not have the ace of hearts (conceivable) his response would have been 6C in which case the opener would have passed or signed off at 6H.

## Summary of the Two Club Opening

When playing Weak Twos the only forcing opening bid is 2C. There are at least three ways to respond to this opening bid and you and your partner should discuss which one best suits the partnership.

If the 2C opener rebids either 2NT or 3NT the responder takes charge. Most experts play the same way over no trump rebids as they would if their partner had opened 2NT or 3NT, the only difference being they know partner has 22-24 if the rebid is 2NT and 27-28 if the rebid is 3NT. The opening bid of 2NT is 20-22 and an opening bid of 3NT is 25-26.

If the opening bidder shows a suit at his first opportunity the partnership is forced to game (unless the partnership makes agreements to the contrary).

Single jump responses to an opening 2C bid are best used to show one loser suits and double jump responses to show solid suits. Playing 2D as the negative response (Method III) a jump response of 3D simply shows a positive response in diamonds and not necessarily a one loser suit.

A jump to 4C over 2C should show a solid suit rather than a one loser suit as it is easier to remember that all jumps to the four level show solid suits.

## Something New

If the 2C opener makes a jump rebid after a 2D response, he shows a solid suit and requests partner to cue bid any ace he may have.

If the responder has no ace, no king, and no side suit singleton, he must raise opener's suit, even with a void!

If the responder has a side suit king or singleton, he rebids 3NT. Opener can now make an asking bid, if he wishes, to discover if responder has the right king or the right singleton. (See Asking Bids pp. 90-91).

| Opener | Responder | Opener | Responder |
|---|---|---|---|
| S. AKQJ876 | S. 3 | 2C | 2D |
| H. - | H. J987654 | 3S | 3NT |
| D. AQJ4 | D. K2 | 4D | 4NT |
| C. AK | C. 1054 | 7S | Pass |

Opener shows a solid suit and responder shows a side suit king or singleton with the 3NT rebid. Opener bids 4D, an asking bid, and responder shows the king of diamonds. Voila, opener need hear no more.

## Something Newer

Another possible meaning for a jump rebid by the opener after a 2D response is to show a hugh three-suiter, the opener jumping in the singleton or void suit!

| Opener | Responder | Opener | Responder |
|---|---|---|---|
| S. AKJ5 | S. 32 | 2C | 2D |
| H. 2 | H. QJ943 | 3H | 3NT |
| D. AKQ6 | D. 543 | Pass | |
| C. AQJ5 | C. 1076 | | |

Opener shows a gigantic three-suiter (upwards of 22/23 high card points), and responder signs off at 3NT. Having shown the entire hand with the 3H rebid, opener passes.

This variation works particularly well when the opener has a singleton heart or spade as the jump keeps the partnership beneath 3NT.

Even so, when not playing a 2D opening to show a strong three-suiter, these hands are practically unbiddable. In my opinion,it is more important to be able to show a strong three-suited hand than it is to show a solid suit.

## NEW MATERIAL FOR SECOND EDITION OF THIS BOOK

They say that confession is good for the soul. All right,
I confess. In the first edition of this book, I did not
give enough space to some conventions that are certainly
worthy of more than a paragraph or two.

Your constructive suggestions have been appreciated and
the new additions in this book will be a bonus to all those
who adore Non-Forcing Stayman, Two-Way Stayman, Gambling
Three No Trump Openings, Flannery Extensions and Splinter Bids.

I look forward to your comments and suggestions, as well as
hearing about interesting hands where you have utilized some
of the bridge conventions discussed in this book. Write me
in care of my publisher, Wilshire Book Company, 12015 Sherman
Road, North Hollywood, California 91605.

Yours for better and more enjoyable bridge,

Edwin Kantar

Non Forcing Stayman appears to be the most popular of all the Stayman variations. Below a workable method for the convention is presented although other versions exist.

| Opener | Responder | Meaning of Responder's Final Bid |
|---|---|---|
| 1NT | 2C | Asking opener to name a four card major. Generally promising at least 7 HCP. Opener denies a major by re-bidding two diamonds. |
| 1NT<br>2D | 2C<br>2H,2S | Not forcing. Promises a five card suit (could be six) and 6-8 HCP. (With a six card suit responder needs only 5-6 HCP). Opener passes unless he holds a maximum plus a fit for responder. |
| 1NT<br>2D | 2C<br>Pass | Responder has apparently used Stayman with a singleton or void in clubs and support for each of the other suits. A typical hand: S.K765 H.J876 D.J9876 C.Void. |
| 1NT<br>2D,2H,2S | 2C<br>2NT | Not forcing. Responder has 8-9 HCP with either one or two four card majors and was unable to locate a major suit fit. Responder is unlikely to hold a five card major on this sequence, with the possible exception of a five card heart suit that he was unable to show over a two spade response. |
| 1NT<br>2D,2H,2S | 2C<br>3NT | 10-14 HCP and no five card major. |
| 1NT<br>2D,2H,2S | 2C<br>3C,3D | This sequence is best used to invite game if partner has a fit for the minor plus a maximum, or near maximum. Two possible hands:<br>1. S.KJ43 H.4 D.54 C.Q108765<br>2. S.Q76 H.54 D.KJ10876 C.J5 |

Notice that responder need not have a
four card major to respond 2C and then
rebid three of a minor.

|      |      |
|------|------|
|      | 2C   |
| 2S   | 3H   |

If responder does have a four card
major in addition to his long minor,
and opener bids that major, responder
simply raises, concealing his minor.

| 1NT  | 2C   |
| 2S   | 3H   |

A 3H REBID BY RESPONDER OVER 2S IS
FORCING TO GAME.

| 1NT  | 2C      |
| 2D   | 3H,3S   |

A FIVE CARD SUIT with game values.
Forcing.  If opener is maximum with a
three card fit he cue bids a control
rather than raising directly to game.
If responder has slam intentions (possible), he will know opener is interested if he hears opener cue bid.
With a doubleton in responder's major,
opener rebids 3NT.

| 1NT  | 2D,2H,2S |

Signoffs.

| 1NT  | 3C,3D,3H,3S |

Slam tries with six card suits.
Typically 13-15 HCP.  Using this method
there is no signoff in clubs.  With a
club bust PASS and run to clubs if
someone doubles.  You can't have everything.

| 1NT  | 4C   |

Gerber.

| 1NT  | 4H,4S |

Signoffs

| 1NT  | 4NT  |

Natural.  Can be passed if opener is
minimum.  If opener is maximum he can
mention his cheapest four card suit if
the hand contains a doubleton.  Responder does the same, and a 4-4 fit might
be uncovered before settling in six no
trump.

| 1NT        | 2C   |
| 2D,2H,2S   | 4C   |

Gerber

108

| Opener | Responder | Natural.  Can be passed if opener is |
|---|---|---|
| 1NT | 2C | minimum.  Opener, if maximum can mention |
| 2D,2H,2♠ | 4NT | his lowest unbid four card suit. |

Perhaps the major drawback to playing Non Forcing Stayman without
Jacoby Transfers is the handling of game-going minor-major two-suiters.

Assume as responder you hold:  S. AQ765  H. 54  D. KJ984  C. 2

| Opener | Responder (you) |
|---|---|
| 1NT | 2C |
| 2D | ? |

Playing Forcing Stayman you can bid 2♠ and if partner rebid 2NT you can
conveniently show your diamonds beneath the level of 3NT.  Playing
Non Forcing Stayman you must leap to 3♠ and if partner rebids 3NT
you must guess whether or not to show the diamonds.

The truth of the matter is that playing Non Forcing Stayman you should
be playing Jacoby Transfers as well.  In that case a transfer followed
by new suit is always considered forcing.

### SMOLEN

When playing non-forcing Stayman in conjunction with the Jacoby
Transfer, Smolen comes in very handy.

| Opener | Responder | Opener | Responder |
|---|---|---|---|
| 1NT | 2C | S. A4 | S. Q763 |
| 2D | 3S | H. K105 | H. QJ832 |
| 4H | Pass | D. Q876 | D. A |
|  |  | C. AKJ4 | C. 976 |

A 2C response followed by a <u>jump</u> to three of a major shows a
5-4 major suit hand, the jump coming in the four card suit. This allows
the opener with three cards in responder's five card major to become
the declarer.

Give the responder five spades, four hearts and a game forcing
response, and he would first bid 2C and then <u>jump</u> to three hearts
to show  that precise distribution.

Yet another version of Stayman that is enjoying increasing popularity is Two Way Stayman. Again, there exist many treatments. Expert intricacies will be saved until the end of this section and are optional at best.

| Opener | Responder | Meaning of Responder's Last Bid |
|---|---|---|
| 1NT | 2C | This response is used to begin all INVITATIONAL SEQUENCES. In other words, game is possible from the responder's point of view only if opener is maximum with a fit for responder's suit. |

| Opener | Responder | This response is FORCING TO GAME. |
|---|---|---|
| 1NT | 2D | Responder might even have slam in mind, but under no circumstances must opener pass before game is reached. |

Opener denies a four card major by rebidding 2D over 2C or 2NT over 2D.

| Opener | Responder | Responder has a weak hand with a |
|---|---|---|
| 1NT | 2C | singleton or void in clubs and |
| 2D | Pass | support for each of the other suits. |

| Opener | Responder | Responder has either a five card suit |
|---|---|---|
| 1NT | 2C | with 6-8 HCP or a six card suit with |
| 2D | 2H,2S | 5-6/7HCP. (Some 7 point hands leap to 4H or 4S.) |

| Opener | Responder | Responder has 8-9 HCP and no fit |
|---|---|---|
| 1NT | 2C | with opener's major. Same point |
| 2D,2H,2S | 2NT | range as a direct raise to 2NT. |

| Opener | Responder | Responder has either a hand with a |
|---|---|---|
| 1NT | 2C | four card major and a five or six |
| 2D,2H,2S | 3C,3D | card minor, or a broken minor one suiter that needs a fit for game:<br>1.S.5  H.K876 D.54 C.A107654<br>2.S.65 H.654 D.AJ9854 C.J10 |

| Opener | Responder | This sequence shows a five card suit. |
|---|---|---|
| 1NT | 2C | Not forcing. Typically 8-9 HCP. |
| 2S | 3H | With a weaker hand responder rebids 2NT, concealing his suit. |

| Opener | Responder | Responder invites game; opener |
|---|---|---|
| 1NT | 2C | proceeds with a maximum. |
| 2H | 3H | |

| Opener | Responder | Responder shows a five card suit and |
|---|---|---|
| 1NT | 2D | is forcing to game. |
| 2H | 2S | |

| Opener | Responder | Meaning of Responder's Last Bid(cont'd) |
|---|---|---|
| 1NT<br>2S | 2D<br>**3H** | Five card suit. Forcing to game. |

| Opener | Responder | |
|---|---|---|
| 1NT<br>2H,2S | 2D<br>2NT | Looking for more information. Opener shows a second suit or rebids **a** five card major suit. |

| Opener | Responder | |
|---|---|---|
| 1NT<br>2H,2S,2NT | 2D<br>3C,3D | Usually a minor suit slam try. The only other possibility is a hand with a four card major and a five or six card minor. If the responder has a five card minor he should have a singleton or something extra to use this sequence. Possible hands:<br>1. S.A5 H.A54 D.3 C.KJ109654<br>2. S.QJ87 H.2 D.AJ10876 C.Q5<br>With: S.KQ76 H.54 D.65 C.AK654,<br>respond 2D but then rebid 3NT if partner does not bid spades. |

| Opener | Responder | |
|---|---|---|
| 1NT | 2H,2S,4H,4S | All signoffs. |

| Opener | Responder | |
|---|---|---|
| 1NT | 3C,3D | Signoffs. |

| Opener | Responder | |
|---|---|---|
| 1NT | 3H,3S | Slam tries with six or seven card suits. With five card suits, responder bids 2D first. |

| Opener | Responder | |
|---|---|---|
| 1NT | 4C | Gerber |

| Opener | Responder | |
|---|---|---|
| 1NT | 4NT | Natural. Not forcing. Not Blackwood. |

| Opener | Responder | |
|---|---|---|
| 1NT<br>2H,2S,2NT | 2D<br>4C | Gerber |

| Opener | Responder | |
|---|---|---|
| 1NT<br>2H,2S,2NT | 2D<br>4NT | Natural. Not forcing. Not Blackwood. |

# Expert Ideas and Innovations With Regard To Two Way Stayman

1.  Since a response of either two clubs or two diamonds can easily be doubled for a lead, it is possible when holding a game going hand that is weak in diamonds (e.g.,S.KQ76 H.AJ43 D.2 C.8765) to fool partner with a response of <u>two clubs</u>, intending to raise to game if partner mentions a major or rebid three no trump if he does not. This avoids the possibility of some nasty opponent making a lead-directing double of an original two diamond response.

2.  The following sequence lends itself to many ideas:

| Opener | Responder |
|--------|-----------|
| 1NT | 2D |
| 2H | 3H |

As long as the two diamond response is forcing to game and responder has four hearts why doesn't he simply raise to game?

Idea I.   Responder has 4-3-3-3 distribution with four hearts. If opener has the same distribution, no trump is likely to play better. Opener rebids 3NT if he too has 4-3-3-3. (Of course, this applies to spades as well.)

Idea II.  Responder is making a slam try in hearts. If opener likes his hand he should cue bid rather than woodenly say four hearts.

Idea III. Combines I and II. Opener assumes responder is 4-3-3-3 and rebids 3NT with a similar distribution. However, if opener has any other shape he assumes partner is making a slam try and cue bids with a maximum. If responder had no slam interest his next bid must be four of the agreed major suit.

3.

| Opener | Responder | |
|--------|-----------|---|
| 1NT | 2D | What does responder mean when he |
| 2H | 3S,4C,4D | jumps after an original 2D response, which is already forcing to game? |

An idea that seems to have considerable merit is for responder's jump to promise a fit with opener's suit, a slam interest, and a <u>singleton</u> in the jump suit.

| Opener | Responder | | Opener | Responder |
|--------|-----------|---|--------|-----------|
| S.AQ76 | S.KJ54 | | 1NT | 2D |
| H.765 | H.2 | | 2S | 4H |
| D.KQ4 | D.A10832 | | 4NT | 5D |
| C.AQ6 | C.K84 | | 6S | Pass |

Upon discovering that responder is interested in a spade slam holding a singleton heart, opener, with all the right cards, is off to the races.

For those who feel cheated out of their Jacoby sequences when they play Two Way Stayman, do not despair. We have something for you.

| Opener | Responder | Meaning of Responder's Last Bid |
|---|---|---|
| 1NT | 4C | Transfer to 4H |
| 1NT | 4D | Transfer to 4S |
| 1NT 4H | 4C 4NT | Blackwood, with hearts the agreed suit. |
| 1NT 4S | 4D 4NT | Blackwood, with spades the agreed suit. Notice that opener plays the hand in both cases. Also.... |
| 1NT 2D,2H,2S | 2C 4C | Gerber, with clubs the agreed suit. |
| 1NT 2H,2S,2NT | 2C 4D | Gerber, with diamonds the agreed suit. Enough? |

A form of Two Way Stayman can also be used over a <u>2NT</u> opening, but it is rarely used. Basically, it goes like this: Responses of both 3C and 3D are forcing to game but the 3D response indicates slam interest.

Therefore, the sequence:

| | Opener | Responder | |
|---|---|---|---|
| | 2NT | 3D | |
| | 3H | 4H | ...is a slam try. |

# BLACKWOOD WITH A VOID (For Experts)

The method given on page 33 can be improved upon. This is the update:

1. With <u>zero</u> or <u>two</u> aces and a void respond 5NT.
THIS ASSUMES THAT FROM THE PREVIOUS BIDDING YOUR PARTNER WILL
BE ABLE TO TELL WHETHER YOU HAVE A REASONABLE HAND, IN WHICH
CASE HE WILL COUNT ON YOU FOR TWO ACES, OR A WEAK HAND, IN WHICH
CASE HE WILL PLAY YOU FOR NO ACES. <u>CAUTION</u>: If you have no aces
and a void in a suit <u>previously bid by partner</u>, respond 5C rather
than 5NT.

| Opener | **Responder** | | Opener | Responder |
|--------|-----------|--|--------|-----------|
| S.AK105432 | S.Q76 | | 2C | 2D* |
| H.AK | H.76543 | | 2S | 3S |
| D.AK | D.108542 | | 4NT | 5NT** |
| C.K5 | C.None | | 6C*** | 6S**** |
| | | | 7S***** | Pass****** |

\*      A known weak hand.

\*\*     Either zero or two aces plus a void. In this case opener
knows from both his own hand and partner's previous bidding that responder has no aces.

\*\*\*    Which suit is your void? This little void-asking conven-
tion works best if spades is the agreed suit.

\*\*\*\*   With a diamond or heart void the responder would bid his
void. With a club void he bids six spades.

\*\*\*\*\* Ain't we terrific?

\*\*\*\*\*\* Yes.

2. With one or three aces and a void, jump to six of the void
suit if it is lower ranking than the agreed suit, and jump to six
of the agreed suit if the void is higher ranking than the agreed
suit. Again the previous bidding is supposed to be explicit
enough for partner to know whether you are showing one or three
aces.

| Opener | Responder | | Opener | Responder |
|--------|-----------|--|--------|-----------|
| S.A1052 | S.KQ9843 | | 1D | 1S |
| H.None | H.10976 | | 3H* | 4NT |
| D.AQ8765 | D.K2 | | 6H** | 7S*** |
| C.A54 | C.3 | | | |

\* Splinter jump showing a powerful hand with four card spade support and a singleton (or possibly a void), in the jump suit.

\*\* Showing either one or three aces plus a heart void.

\*\*\* Responder knows that opener's previous bidding has been strong, so he assumes three aces plus a heart void and bids the grand slam.

### Exclusion Roman Key Card Blackwood (ERKCB)

This is one of my babies. After a major suit agreement at the three level, a jump over game (usually by the opener), shows a void and asks partner for key cards excluding the ace of the jump suit.

| Opener | Responder | Opener | Responder |
|--------|-----------|--------|-----------|
| S. AQ10543 | S. KJ97 | 1S | 3S\* |
| H. KQ105 | ♡ 42 | 5C\*\* | 5H\*\*\* |
| D. KQ6 | ◊ 1075 | 5S | Pass |
| ♣ - | ♣ AQ76 | | |

```
  * Limit Raise
 ** ERKCB
*** One key card outside of clubs.
```

Opener knows that the hand is missing two key cards and signs off in 5S. Had responder a red ace instead of the Ace of clubs he would respond 5S showing two key cards, and opener would bid the slam.

If the opener wishes to ask for kings, he bids six of the void suit. The responder does not count the king of the void suit when responding.

## ODDS AND ENDS
### FLANNERY

Playing Flannery and having opened with 2D to show five hearts and four spades and typically 12-15 HCP, responder's first bid of 2NT is forcing and asks for distributional clarification.

If opener is 3-1 in the minors he rebids his three card suit (or his singleton). (In the text, page 81, he rebids his three card suit although many experts rebid the singleton.) The new idea is with 4-5-2-2 distribution responder has three possible rebids over two no trump:

1.  3H        Showing a minimum point count -- 11-13 HCP.
2.  3S        Showing 14-15 HCP, most of them concentrated in the
                  major suits.
3.  3NT       Showing 14-15 HCP with at least 6 HCP in the minors.

This means that opener does not toy with Flannery holding four spades and six hearts, a doubtful practice at best.

### THE GAMBLING THREE NO TRUMP OPENING BID

This convention was not mentioned in the original text, but it is fairly widely played in tournament bridge and deserves some discussion. Basically, there are two ways to handle this opening bid.

1.  An opening bid of 3NT shows a seven or eight card solid minor suit and no ace or king on the outside. In other words, you are really gambling. If someone doubles and partner passes you are supposed to stick out the double as partner knows you have no other suit stopped. Excitement!
    If partner removes to 4C you are supposed to pass if clubs is your suit and correct to 4D if it is diamonds. Responses of 4H and 4S are to play, whether the opponents double or not. A response of 4D asks you to pass if diamonds is your suit but to bid 5C if clubs is.

2.  The second version requires a six or seven card solid minor suit with at least two of the other three suits stopped.
    Typical hands are:   S.4 H.K54 D.A3 C.AKQ7654
                                 S.K2 H.82 D.AKQJ98 C.K54

    The opponents are less apt to double, but on the other hand you are more apt to be in the wrong spot, for partner does not have as much specific information about your hand. If

you have a weak heart perhaps it is best to play the second
version; if you crave thrills - try the first.

Note:  Playing either way, you must open 2C and then rebid 3NT
with your strong balanced hands in the 25-27 range.

# SPLINTER JUMPS

The key to bidding most suit slams that are short in point count is distribution. If one player has a good fit with his partner's last bid suit plus a singleton or void and some slam interest there should be a way to convey this message below the slam level. The answer is to use either Splinter or Fragment Jumps to show partner your short suit so that he can evaluate the combined hands for slam purposes.

Using Splinter Jumps one player makes an unusual jump which by agreement indicates a four card fit or greater with partner's last bid suit, a singleton (usually) or a void (possibly) in the jump suit and slam interest.

Splinter Jumps can be made by either the opener or responder. In order to make a Splinter Jump, opener jumps one level higher than a jump shift or makes a jump reverse. Responder does like-wise.

Before listing a chart which contains most opener and responder splinter sequences, here are a few examples. First, Splinter Jumps by opener:

| Opener | Responder |   | Opener | Responder |
|--------|-----------|---|--------|-----------|
| S.2 | S.KQ54 |   | 1D | 1H |
| H.AK54 | H.Q8763 |   | 3S | 4H |
| D.KQ1087 | D.32 |   | Pass | |
| C.A54 | C.J10 |   | | |

Opener jumps one level higher than a regular jump shift (two spades) to show the singleton spade with heart support and game values. Responder, with wasted spade values, is not interested. And another age-old confusion is removed:

| Opener | Responder |   | Opener | Responder |
|--------|-----------|---|--------|-----------|
| S.2 | S.Q4 |   | 1D | 1H |
| H.A54 | H.Q987 |   | 3C | 4C |
| D.AKJ76 | D.102 |   | 4H | ? |
| C.AQ109 | C.K8765 |   | | |

In olden times responder would not know how many hearts opener was showing, three or four. But using Splinter Jumps responder knows that opener has only three and therefore has an easy correction to five clubs.

A jump reverse is considered to be a Splinter Jump because a simple reverse creates a one round force thus making the jump reverse as a natural forcing bid obsolescent.

| Opener | Responder |
|--------|-----------|
| S.A654 | S.K109732 |
| H.2 | H.A874 |
| D.KQ10 | D.2 |
| C.AKJ76 | C.54 |

| Opener | Responder |
|--------|-----------|
| 1C | 1S |
| 3H | 4H |
| 4S | 4NT |
| 5H | 6S |
| Pass | |

Opener leaps to three hearts (a Jump reverse) to show the singleton heart plus the spade fit. Responder cue bids four hearts to show a slam interest. Opener, sensing that the hand is missing the ace of diamonds and having minimum trump support returns to four spades. Responder, however, has too good a hand and carries on to slam.

The corollary to this sequence is:

| Opener | Responder |
|--------|-----------|
| S.A54 | S.108732 |
| H.2 | H.AKQ |
| D.AQJ7 | D.1054 |
| C.AK843 | C.92 |

| Opener | Responder |
|--------|-----------|
| 1C | 1S |
| 2D | 2NT |
| 3S | 3NT |
| Pass | |

In this sequence opener is also showing a singleton heart but only three card spade support because of his failure to make a direct jump raise or a Splinter Jump. Responder with poor spades and super hearts elects to play three no trump in spite of the known singleton in partner's hand.

Now for some examples of responder making a Splinter Jump.

A.  After opener rebids his original suit.

| Opener | Responder | Opener | Responder |
|--------|-----------|--------|-----------|
| S.4 | S.AK765 | 1H | 1S |
| H.AQJ765 | H.K93 | 2H | 4D |
| D.A76 | D.2 | 4NT | 5H |
| C.Q43 | C.A765 | 6H | |

Responder's leap to four diamonds indicates a singleton diamond, at least three card support (opener has rebid the suit)
and some slam interest, particularly if the hands fit well.

Opener, with the perfect holding in diamonds opposite a singleton, good trumps and good distribution, accepts.

The corollary:

| Opener | Responder | Opener | Responder |
|--------|-----------|--------|-----------|
| S.3 | S.AK765 | 1H | 1S |
| H.AJ10543 | H.K93 | 2H | 3C |
| D.QJ5 | D.32 | 3NT | 4H |
| C.KQ3 | C.AJ9 | Pass | |

This responding sequence also shows slam interest in hearts but
denies a singleton diamond. (No Splinter Jump)  In fact, this
sequence usually promises a small doubleton in diamonds.  Opener,
armed with that information, need not be tempted.

B.  An unusual jump after opener REBIDS a major suit at the one
level.

| Opener | Responder | Opener | Responder |
|--------|-----------|--------|-----------|
| S.AQ87 | S.KJ104 | 1C | 1H |
| H.2 | H.AQJ54 | 1S | 4D* |
| D.KQ5 | D.3 | 4S | |
| C.Q10765 | C.K42 | | |

Responder leaps one level higher than a second round jump shift
(three diamonds) to indicate the singleton.  Opener, with the
"wrong hand" signs off.  In this sequence a leap to four clubs
by the responder shows a singleton club!  This is the only Splinter
Jump sequence where the responder can jump to show a singleton in
a bid suit.  However, in order to make a Splinter Jump in a bid suit
there must be no interference bidding.  If there is, any jump in
partner's suit is natural.

*  There is a very good reason why 4D should be considered the
Splinter Jump as opposed to 3D.  True, a rebid of 2D would be
forcing so that 3D could serve as the Splinter Jump, but it is
better to reserve a second round responder jump (from a higher
ranking suit to a lower ranking one) to show a forcing to game two
suiter, so as to avoid ambiguity with weaker two suiters.

| Opener | Responder (a) | Responder (b) |
|--------|---------------|---------------|
| S.AK76 | S.4 | S.4 |
| H.3 | H.AQ1086 | H.AJ943 |
| D.862 | D.AKJ43 | D.KQ953 |
| C.KQ1043 | C.72 | C.72 |

120

| Opener | Responder (a) | Responder shows a forcing to game red two-suiter (at least 5-5) and opener tries 3NT. |
|--------|---------------|----------------------------------------|
| 1C | 1H | |
| 1S | 3D | |
| 3NT | Pass | |

| Opener | Responder (b) | This time responder also shows a red two-suiter but by failing to jump the second time to 3D he indicates that he does not have game forcing values. Responder, with a minimum, calls it a day. |
|--------|---------------|----------------------------------------|
| 1C | 1H | |
| 1S | 2D | |
| 2NT | 3D | |
| Pass | | |

C.  After an artificial two club opening, a two diamond response (negative), a suit rebid by opener and a jump by responder.

| Opener | Responder | Opener | Responder |
|--------|-----------|--------|-----------|
| S.Q105 | S.2 | 2C | 2D |
| H.AK9876 | H.J1054 | 2H | 3S |
| D.AKQ | D.1065 | 4NT | 5C |
| C.A | C.QJ876 | 6H | Pass |

Responder's second round jump to three spades shows a singleton spade plus a substantial heart fit.  Opener checks for aces (responder might have a singleton ace or perhaps a spade void) and settles down comfortably in the near laydown contract of six hearts.

If responder really had a spade suit he either bids two spades directly over two clubs or with a weaker hand two spades over two hearts.  A second round leap to three spades is hardly necessary to show spades.  However, a direct leap to three spades over two clubs is a natural bid showing a powerful (usually a one-loser) suit.

### SUMMARY OF SPLINTER JUMPS
### BY BOTH OPENER AND RESPONDER

I.  BY OPENER (LAST BID BY OPENER IS A SPLINTER JUMP)

| OPENER | RESPONDER |
|--------|-----------|
| 1C | 1D |
| 3H,3S | |
| 1C | 1H |
| 3D,3S | |
| 1C | 1S |
| 3D,3H | |
| 1D | 1H |
| 3S,4C | |
| 1D | 2C |
| 3H,3S | |
| 1H | 1S |
| 4C,4D | |
| 1H | 2C |
| 3S,4D | |
| 1H | 2D |
| 3S,4C | |

| OPENER | RESPONDER |
|--------|-----------|
| 1S<br>4D,4H | 2C |
| 1S<br>4C,4H | 2D |
| 1S<br>4C,4D | 2H |

**B. BY RESPONDER (LAST BID BY RESPONDER IS A SPLINTER JUMP.)**

| OPENER | RESPONDER | |
|--------|-----------|---|
| 1C<br>1H | 1D<br>3S,4C | |
| 1C<br>1S | 1D<br>3H,4C | |
| 1C<br>2C | 1D<br>3H,3S | |
| 1C<br>1S | 1H<br>4C,4D | Rare sequence where respond-er can jump to show single-ton in a bid suit. |
| 1C<br>2C | 1H<br>3S,4D | 3D would be a natural jump. (Higher ranking to lower ranking suit.) |
| 1C<br>2D | 1H<br>3S | |
| 1C<br>2C | 1S<br>4D,4H | 3D and 3H would be natural jumps. |
| 1C<br>2D | 1S<br>4H | A strong case could be made for 3H to be Splinter Jump after opener reverses. |
| 1C<br>2H | 1S<br>4D | |
| 1D<br>1S | 1H<br>4C,4D | Rare sequence where respond-er can jump to show a single-ton in a bid suit. |
| 1D<br>2C | 1H<br>3S | |
| 1D<br>2D | 1H<br>3S,4C | |
| 1D<br>2C | 1S<br>4H | 3H would be a natural jump. |
| 1D<br>2D | 1S<br>4H | 3H would be a natural jump. |
| 1D<br>2H | 1S<br>4C | |
| 1D<br>2H | 2C<br>3S | |
| 1D<br>2S | 2C<br>4H | |

122

| Opener | Responder | |
|--------|-----------|---|
| 1H     | 1S        | |
| 2C     | 4D        | |
|        |           | |
| 1H     | 1S        | |
| 2D     | 4C        | |
|        |           | |
| 1H     | 2C        | |
| 2D     | 3S        | |
|        |           | |
| 1H     | 2C        | |
| 2H     | 3S,4D     | |
|        |           | |
| 1H     | 2C        | |
| 2S     | 4D        | |
|        |           | |
| 1H     | 2D        | |
| 2H     | 3S,4C     | |
|        |           | |
| 1H     | 2D        | |
| 2S     | 4C        | |
|        |           | |
| 1H     | 2D        | |
| 3C     | 4S        | |
|        |           | |
| 1S     | 2C        | 3H would be a natural |
| 2D     | 3H        | jump. |
|        |           | |
| 1S     | 2C        | |
| 2H     | 4D        | |
|        |           | |
| 1S     | 2C        | |
| 2S     | 4D,4H     | |
|        |           | |
| 1S     | 2D        | |
| 2H     | 4C        | |
|        |           | |
| 1S     | 2D        | |
| 2S     | 4C,4H     | |
|        |           | |
| 1S     | 2D        | |
| 3C     | 4H        | |
|        |           | |
| 1S     | 2H        | |
| 2S     | 4C,4D     | |
|        |           | |
| 1S     | 2H        | |
| 3C     | 4D        | |
|        |           | |
| 2C     | 2D        | |
| 2H     | 3S,4C,4D  | |
|        |           | |
| 2C     | 2D        | |
| 2S     | 4C,4D,4H  | |
|        |           | |
| 2C     | 2D        | |
| 3C     | 4D,4H,4S  | |
|        |           | |
| 2C     | 2D        | |
| 3D     | 4H,4S,5C  | |

# CONCLUSION

To repeat, Fragment Jumps are the same as Splinter Jumps with one exception -- Fragment Jumps are in the unbid side suit to show a singleton in the fourth suit. Therefore, holding: S.AK765 H.AQ76 D.2 C.A54    you open 1S, and assume partner responds 2H. Playing Splinter Jumps you leap to 4D but playing Fragment Jumps you leap to 4C. There is little to choose between the two but to make it easier on your memory you should play either one way or the other but not a little bit of both!

Once you start to play these unusual jumps to show singletons you will find that there are many idle sequences which can be put to work by playing these unusual jumps. For example:

| Opener | Responder |
|--------|-----------|
| 1C     | 1H        |
| 2H     | 3S!       |

Why couldn't responder hold a hand like?  S.2  H.AJ876  D.AQ76 C.K54.   These hands frequently match up for slam but are practically unbiddable playing standard methods. Opener could have: S.654  H.KQ3  D.K4  C.AQ1087.  Slam is a veritable laydown in two suits.

## RESPONDING TO SPLINTER JUMPS

Basically, you should cue bid if you are interested in a slam, return to the original trump suit at the GAME LEVEL if you have no interest whatsoever (but if possible return to the trump suit beneath the game level to show good trumps and nothing else).

| Opener | Responder(a) | Responder(b) |
|--------|--------------|--------------|
| S.K543 | S.AQJ76      | S.QJ862      |
| H.2    | H.765        | H.Q87        |
| D.A43  | D.76         | D.Q76        |
| C.AKQJ4| C.1083       | C.76         |

| Opener | Responder(a) |   |
|--------|--------------|---|
| 1C     | 1S           |   |
| 3H     | 3S           | ...I have good spades but nothing else. |
| 4NT    | 5D           | (Two of the top three honors usually |
| 6S     | Pass         | five long or better.) |

| Opener | Responder(b) |   |
|--------|--------------|---|
| 1C     | 1S           |   |
| 3H     | 4S           | ...I have no slam interest whatsoever. |
| Pass   |              |   |

If either opener or responder rebids three no trump over a fragment jump, that announces weak trumps and two or three stoppers in partner's singleton suit. In other words he is prepared to play three no trump.

THE WESTERN CUE BID

The "Western Cue Bid" is a bid in the opponent's suit, usually made by the opener or the responder at his second opportunity.  The bid asks partner for a stopper in the opponent's suit.

The most common occurrence is after opener and responder have agreed upon a minor suit and are looking for no trump.

For example:  Opener (South)        Responder (North)
               S. xx                 S. Qxx
               H. Axx                H. xx
               D. Axx                D. KQx
               C. AKQxx              C. J10xxx

South    West      North     East
1C       1S        2C        Pass
2S       Pass      2NT       Pass
3NT      All Pass

Also:         Opener (South)        Responder (North)
               S. KQx                S. xx
               H. KQx                H. Ax
               D. xx                 D. J10xx
               C. AJxxx              C. KQxxx

South    West      North     East
1C       1D        3C        Pass
3D       Pass      3NT       All Pass

In both cases there has been an overcall followed by minor suit agreement.  Opener, rather than make ambiguous bids in non-suits, simply bids the opponent's suit asking for a stopper in that suit.  If responder has no stopper, he can either cue bid a feature, return to the trump suit at a minimum level, or jump in the trump suit.

Here are two other familiar situations:

              Opener (South)        Responder (North)
               S. Q10x               S. xxx
               H. xx                 H. Ax
               D. AJxxx              D. Kx
               C. AKx                C. QJ10xxx

Case I.    South    West      North     East
           1D       1S        2C        Pass
           3C       Pass      3S        Pass
           3NT      All Pass

Responder asks for a spade stop, finds one and all is well.

Case II.

| South | West | North | East |
|-------|------|-------|------|
| 1D | 1S | 2C | 2H |
| 3C | Pass | 3H | Pass |
| 3NT | All Pass | | |

In this case the opponents have bid _two_ suits, so the responder bids the suit he has stopped, which is another way of asking partner to bid no trump if he has the other suit stopped.

In other words, if the responder had bid three spades in the second sequence he would be showing a spade stop, not asking for one. When the opponents have bid _two_ suits, you don't ask, you tell!

Sometimes the player asked for a stopper doesn't have one.

| Opener (South) | Responder (North) |
|----------------|-------------------|
| S. Q10x | S. Kxx |
| H. xx | H. xx |
| D. AJxxx | D. KQ |
| C. AKx | C. QJ10xxx |

| South | West | North | East |
|-------|------|-------|------|
| 1D | 1H | 2C | 2H |
| 3C | Pass | 3H | Pass |
| 4C | All Pass | | |

Responder asks opener for a heart stop. Opener declines showing a minimum at the same time. Responder can count two quick heart losers and should realize that opener cannot have all of the missing key cards (ace of spades, ace of diamonds, ace-king of clubs) and only return to four clubs. With all those goodies he would surely cue bid the ace of spades or jump to five clubs.

Playing four card major suit openings there are cases where the Western Cue Bid can be made after major suit agreement:

| Opener (South) | Responder (North) |
|----------------|-------------------|
| S. xxx | S. Kx |
| H. AKxx | H. Qxx |
| D. AQxx | D. KJ10xx |
| C. Qx | C. Jxx |

```
               South     West      North     East
               1H        1S        2D        2S
               3D        Pass      3H        Pass
               3S        Pass      3NT       All Pass
```

Of course, some players simply open the South hand 1NT, receive
a raise to 3NT, and that's that. However, a 1NT opening bid on the
South cards does leave something to be desired.

Playing five card major openings there would be less reason to
use the Western Cue Bid after major agreement. One possible reason
would be to ask for half a stopper rather than a full one.
Something like: Qx, Jxx, or 10xxx.

```
       Opener (South)             Responder (North)
       S. Axx                     S. Qx
       H. AKJxx                    H. Qxx
       D. xx                       D. Axxx
       C. Axx                      C. xxxx

       South     West      North     East
       1H        1S        2H        Pass
       2S        Pass      2NT       Pass
       3NT       All Pass
```

Playing five card major openings, South asks for a partial stopper,
gets confirmation and tries for the nine trick game. The two spade
rebid might also be a slam try or game probe. It is ambiguous, but
responder would still bid no trump with half a stopper, waiting for
opener to clarify his intentions.

A player who has made an overcall or his partner may use the
"Western Cue" to advantage. These are the two most common positions:

```
       South (overcaller)         North
       S. Kx                      S. xxx
       H. xxx                     H. AJxx
       D. Qx                      D. A10xx
       C. AQ109xx                 C. Kx

       East      South     West      North
       1S        2C        Pass      2S
       Pass      2NT       Pass      3NT
       Pass      Pass      Pass
```

North's two spade response is a catch-all cue bid but its primary purpose is to discover whether or not South has a spade stop. With a minimum hand and a spade stop, South rebids two no trump. With a stronger overcall and a spade stop, South rebids three no trump. With no spade stopper, South either rebids his suit to show a minimum overcall, bids another suit, or jumps in his own suit to show extra values.

```
South (overcaller)      North
S. xxx                  S. Axx
H. Ax                   H. 109xx
D. Ax                   D. xxx
C. AQ10xxx              C. KJx

East     South    West     North
1S       2C       Pass     3C
Pass     3S       Pass     3NT
Pass     Pass     Pass
```

This time North simply raises the overcall, weaker than either cue bidding or responding two no trump. South, however, has an excellent overcall and needs a spade stop from North.

The three spade bid is asking North to bid three no trump with a spade stopper irrespective of his non-holdings in the other suits. It is not for North to reason why, it is for North to do or die!

# FLINT

This is a convention designed for the responder to be able to sign off at three of a major after partner opens _two_ no trump. (20 - 22)

It works like this: assume for the moment that the responder has a very weak hand with a six card major suit. Perhaps one of these two possible hands:

    a.  S. Jxxxxx  H. x  D. xxx  C. xxx

    b.  S. x  H. Jxxxxx  D. xxx  C. xxx

In either case the response is THREE DIAMONDS. The opener now rebids as follows:

    With a minimum hand for both majors: THREE HEARTS
    With a maximum hand for both majors: THREE NO TRUMP
    With a maximum hand for hearts only: THREE SPADES
    With a maximum hand for spades only: THREE HEARTS

Let's take the various cases:

| Opener | Responder | Opener | Responder |
|--------|-----------|--------|-----------|
| S. Ax | S. Qxxxxx | 2NT | 3D |
| H. KJx | H. xx | 3H | 3S |
| D. KQxx | D. x | Pass | |
| C. KQJx | C. xxxx | | |

Opener rebids 3H to show either a minimum for both majors or a maximum for spades. If responder has hearts, he passes. If responder has spades he converts to three spades which opener passes with a minimum or raises to four with a maximum.

It is conceivable that responder is strong enough to insist on game when he responds three diamonds and is simply using the bid as a form of transfer to get the stronger hand to declare. Thus:

| Opener | Responder | Opener | Responder |
|--------|-----------|--------|-----------|
| S. Ax | S. Kxx | 2NT | 3D |
| H. KJx | H. Q10xxxx | 3H | 4H |
| D. KQxx | D. Jxx | Pass | |
| C. KQJx | C. x | | |

Had opener rebid three spades or three no trump instead of three hearts, responder rebids four hearts which is terminal!

129

Transferring with long spades and a game going hand is also possible, but chances are not quite as good that opener will rebid three spades over three diamonds. In this case responder must bid four spades himself on the rebid, terminal.

| Opener | Responder | Opener | Responder |
|--------|-----------|--------|-----------|
| S. AQx | S. KJxxxx | 2NT | 3D |
| H. Kx | H. xx | 3H | 4S |
| D. AJxx | D. Qxx | Pass | |
| C. KQJx | C. xx | | |

Responder can have two other types of hands to respond three diamonds besides the major signoff or major game going hands. Responder can have a diamond suit slam-try type hand. Something like: S. xx H. xx D. AQxxxx C. Kxx

| Opener | Responder |
|--------|-----------|
| 2NT | 3D |
| 3H or 3S | 3NT |

The rebid of 3NT after the original three diamond response shows a <u>diamond</u> slam try. If opener rebids 3NT over 3D showing a maximum for both majors, responder raises to 4NT, not forcing, to show the hand with the long diamonds.

Finally, responder may have a diamond-club two suiter that has slam possibilities. In that case responder first bids 3D, and over any rebid, 4C.

| | Opener | Responder | Meaning |
|---|---|---|---|
| A. | 2NT<br>3H | 3D<br>Pass | Responder has a weak hand with long hearts.<br>Opener has a minimum for hearts. |
| B. | Opener<br>2NT<br>3H<br>4S | Responder<br>3D<br>3S | Responder has a weak hand with long spades.<br>Opener has a maximum hand for spades,<br>with a minimum he passes three spades. |
| C. | Opener<br>2NT<br>3H | Responder<br>3D<br>4H | Responder has a game-going hand with at<br>least six hearts. (Sign-off) |
| D. | Opener<br>2NT<br>3H | Responder<br>3D<br>4S | Responder has a game-going hand with at<br>least six spades. (Sign-off) |
| E. | Opener<br>2NT<br>3S | Responder<br>3D<br>Pass | Opener has a maximum hand for hearts,<br>responder has a weak hand with spades. |
| F. | Opener<br>2NT<br>3S | Responder<br>3D<br>4H | Opener has a maximum hand for hearts,<br>responder has hearts. |
| G. | Opener<br>2NT<br>3NT | Responder<br>3D<br>4H or 4S | Opener has a maximum for either major<br>and responder signs off in his major. |
| H. | Opener<br>2NT<br>3H, 3S | Responder<br>3D<br>3NT | Responder is making a slam try in diamonds.<br>Note: Responder <u>never</u> makes a slam try in<br>a major by responding three diamonds.<br>The most he can be interested in is<br>game, and usually less! |
| I. | Opener<br>2NT<br>3NT | Responder<br>3D<br>4NT | Responder is making a slam try in diamonds.<br>Opener is allowed to pass 4NT. |
| J. | Opener<br>2NT<br>3H,3S,3NT | Responder<br>3D<br>4C | Responder is showing a strong two suited<br>minor hand. However, if opener rebids 4NT<br>responder is allowed to pass. |

The Flint Convention was originally designed to play in three of a major in response to a two no trump opening bid. However, if you are going to use the convention you might as well get maximum mileage.

(Some of the ideas expressed here are mine (C-D,J) but it is hard to see how any of them conflict with the original concept of the Convention.)

# THE MILES CONVENTION

This is a convention designed to handle 18 and 19 point balanced hands opposite opening bids. Assuming the immediate jump response of 3NT to an opening bid shows 16-17, balanced, how does one show a stronger hand?

In the Miles Convention the responder first bids 2NT, temporarily showing 13-15 balanced, and then 4NT over any rebid partner makes. The rebid of 4NT announces that responder originally had 18-19, balanced. The 4NT rebid is not Blackwood, nor is it forcing.

| Opener | Responder | Opener | Responder |
|--------|-----------|--------|-----------|
| S. Axx | S. KQx | 1D | 2NT |
| H. Kxx | H. AJx | 3NT | 4NT |
| D. Qxxx | D. AJx | Pass | |
| C. Axx | C. Kxxx | | |

Opener with a balanced 13 count wisely decides to pass 4NT, a contract which will make most of the time, but not every time even though there are 31 high card points between the two hands. If opener does bid over responder's quantitative 4NT rebid, he is accepting the slam try. However, opener does not show aces, but rather additional distributional assets, such as naming a new four card suit or rebidding a five card suit.

| Opener | Responder | Opener | Responder |
|--------|-----------|--------|-----------|
| S. Ax | S. Kxx | 1D | 2NT |
| H. Qxx | H. AKx | 3NT | 4NT |
| D. AKxx | D. Qxx | 5C | 6C |
| C. J10xx | C. AQxx | Pass | |

Opener, with slightly more than a minimum and no wasted strength accepts the invitation and shows a second four card suit. Responder with four clubs raises to slam. Six clubs is a superior contract to six no trump, making when the club finesse is wrong and diamonds do not divide, as a spade ruff can be secured for the twelfth trick.

Even if opener accepts the slam invitation, the hand can still play in five no trump if responder is absolutely minimum and there is no eight card fit between the two hands.

| Opener | Responder | Opener | Responder |
|--------|-----------|--------|-----------|
| S. Ax | S. QJxx | 1D | 2NT |
| H. Qxx | H. AKx | 3NT | 4NT |
| D. AKxx | D. Jxx | 5C | 5NT |
| C. J10xx | C. AKx | Pass | |

Responder shows a balanced 18 count by signing off at five no trump. If opener has as much as 14 and a five card suit, or any 15 point hand he is obliged to bid a slam.

If responder has 19 he must never sign off at five no trump, bidding either six no trump or six of one of opener's suits.

If responder cannot bear to play the hand in less than slam holding a gilt-edged 19 or 20, he can first jump to 2NT and then bid 5NT, forcing to slam, at his next opportunity.

Opener must then bid six no trump or name a four card suit if it appears the hand might play better at a suit contract.

| Opener | Responder | Opener | Responder |
|--------|-----------|--------|-----------|
| S. Kxx | S. AJx | 1C | 2NT |
| H. A10x | H. KQx | 3NT | 5NT |
| D. Qxx | D. AKxx | 6NT | Pass |
| C. Axxx | C. QJx | | |

| Opener | Responder | Opener | Responder |
|--------|-----------|--------|-----------|
| S. xx | S. AKx | 1C | 2NT |
| H. AQxx | H. Kxxx | 3NT | 5NT |
| D. Kxx | D. AJx | 6H | Pass |
| C. Axxx | C. KQx | | |

In both cases the proper contract is reached, although it may make some nervous to bid the trump suit for the first time at the six level.

# MELVIN POWERS SELF-IMPROVEMENT LIBRARY

## ASTROLOGY

____ASTROLOGY—HOW TO CHART YOUR HOROSCOPE  Max Heindel . . . . . . . . . . . . . 7.00
____ASTROLOGY AND SEXUAL ANALYSIS  Morris C. Goodman . . . . . . . . . . . . . . 7.00
____ASTROLOGY AND YOU  Carroll Righter . . . . . . . . . . . . . . . . . . . . . . . . 5.00
____ASTROLOGY MADE EASY  Astarte . . . . . . . . . . . . . . . . . . . . . . . . . . 7.00
____ASTROLOGY, ROMANCE, YOU AND THE STARS  Anthony Norvell . . . . . . . . . . . 10.00
____MY WORLD OF ASTROLOGY  Sydney Omarr . . . . . . . . . . . . . . . . . . . . . 10.00
____THOUGHT DIAL  Sydney Omarr . . . . . . . . . . . . . . . . . . . . . . . . . . . 7.00
____WHAT THE STARS REVEAL ABOUT THE MEN IN YOUR LIFE  Thelma White . . . . . . . 3.00

## BRIDGE

____BRIDGE BIDDING MADE EASY  Edwin B. Kantar . . . . . . . . . . . . . . . . . . 15.00
____BRIDGE CONVENTIONS  Edwin B. Kantar . . . . . . . . . . . . . . . . . . . . . 10.00
____COMPETITIVE BIDDING IN MODERN BRIDGE  Edgar Kaplan . . . . . . . . . . . . . 7.00
____DEFENSIVE BRIDGE PLAY COMPLETE  Edwin B Kantar . . . . . . . . . . . . . . . 20.00
____GAMESMAN BRIDGE—PLAY BETTER WITH KANTAR  Edwin B. Kantar . . . . . . . . 7.00
____HOW TO IMPROVE YOUR BRIDGE  Alfred Sheinwold . . . . . . . . . . . . . . . . 7.00
____IMPROVING YOUR BIDDING SKILLS  Edwin B. Kantar . . . . . . . . . . . . . . . . 7.00
____INTRODUCTION TO DECLARER'S PLAY  Edwin B. Kantar . . . . . . . . . . . . . . . 7.00
____INTRODUCTION TO DEFENDER'S PLAY  Edwin B. Kantar . . . . . . . . . . . . . . . 7.00
____KANTAR FOR THE DEFENSE  Edwin B. Kantar . . . . . . . . . . . . . . . . . . . 7.00
____KANTAR FOR THE DEFENSE VOLUME 2  Edwin B. Kantar . . . . . . . . . . . . . . 10.00
____TEST YOUR BRIDGE PLAY  Edwin B. Kantar . . . . . . . . . . . . . . . . . . . . 10.00
____VOLUME 2—TEST YOUR BRIDGE PLAY  Edwin B. Kantar . . . . . . . . . . . . . . 10.00
____WINNING DECLARER PLAY  Dorothy Hayden Truscott . . . . . . . . . . . . . . . 10.00

## BUSINESS, STUDY & REFERENCE

____BRAINSTORMING  Charles Clark . . . . . . . . . . . . . . . . . . . . . . . . . 10.00
____CONVERSATION MADE EASY  Elliot Russell . . . . . . . . . . . . . . . . . . . . 5.00
____EXAM SECRET  Dennis B. Jackson . . . . . . . . . . . . . . . . . . . . . . . . 5.00
____FIX-IT BOOK  Arthur Symons . . . . . . . . . . . . . . . . . . . . . . . . . . . 2.00
____HOW TO DEVELOP A BETTER SPEAKING VOICE  M. Hellier . . . . . . . . . . . . . 5.00
____HOW TO SAVE 50% ON GAS & CAR EXPENSES  Ken Stansbie . . . . . . . . . . . . 5.00
____HOW TO SELF-PUBLISH YOUR BOOK & MAKE IT A BEST SELLER  Melvin Powers . . 20.00
____INCREASE YOUR LEARNING POWER  Geoffrey A. Dudley . . . . . . . . . . . . . . 5.00
____PRACTICAL GUIDE TO BETTER CONCENTRATION  Melvin Powers . . . . . . . . . . 5.00
____PUBLIC SPEAKING MADE EASY  Thomas Montalbo . . . . . . . . . . . . . . . . 10.00
____7 DAYS TO FASTER READING  William S. Schaill . . . . . . . . . . . . . . . . . 7.00
____SONGWRITER'S RHYMING DICTIONARY  Jane Shaw Whitfield . . . . . . . . . . . 10.00
____SPELLING MADE EASY  Lester D. Basch & Dr. Milton Finkelstein . . . . . . . . . . 3.00
____STUDENT'S GUIDE TO BETTER GRADES  J.A. Rickard . . . . . . . . . . . . . . . 3.00
____TEST YOURSELF—FIND YOUR HIDDEN TALENT  Jack Shafer . . . . . . . . . . . . 3.00
____YOUR WILL & WHAT TO DO ABOUT IT  Attorney Samuel G. King . . . . . . . . . . 7.00

## CALLIGRAPHY

____ADVANCED CALLIGRAPHY  Katherine Jeffares . . . . . . . . . . . . . . . . . . . 7.00
____CALLIGRAPHY—THE ART OF BEAUTIFUL WRITING  Katherine Jeffares . . . . . . . 7.00
____CALLIGRAPHY FOR FUN & PROFIT  Anne Leptich & Jacque Evans . . . . . . . . . 7.00
____CALLIGRAPHY MADE EASY  Tina Serafini . . . . . . . . . . . . . . . . . . . . . 7.00

## CHESS & CHECKERS

____BEGINNER'S GUIDE TO WINNING CHESS  Fred Reinfeld . . . . . . . . . . . . . . 10.00
____CHESS IN TEN EASY LESSONS  Larry Evans . . . . . . . . . . . . . . . . . . . 10.00
____CHESS MADE EASY  Milton L. Hanauer . . . . . . . . . . . . . . . . . . . . . . 5.00
____CHESS PROBLEMS FOR BEGINNERS  Edited by Fred Reinfeld . . . . . . . . . . . 7.00

\_\_\_CHESS TACTICS FOR BEGINNERS  Edited by Fred Reinfeld . . . . . . . . . . . . . . . . . . .  7.00
\_\_\_HOW TO WIN AT CHECKERS  Fred Reinfeld . . . . . . . . . . . . . . . . . . . . . . . . . . . . .  7.00
\_\_\_1001 BRILLIANT WAYS TO CHECKMATE  Fred Reinfeld . . . . . . . . . . . . . . . . . . .  10.00
\_\_\_1001 WINNING CHESS SACRIFICES & COMBINATIONS  Fred Reinfeld . . . . . . . . . .  10.00

## COOKERY & HERBS
\_\_\_CULPEPER'S HERBAL REMEDIES  Dr. Nicholas Culpeper . . . . . . . . . . . . . . . . . . .  5.00
\_\_\_FAST GOURMET COOKBOOK  Poppy Cannon . . . . . . . . . . . . . . . . . . . . . . . . . . . .  2.50
\_\_\_HEALING POWER OF HERBS  May Bethel . . . . . . . . . . . . . . . . . . . . . . . . . . . . . .  5.00
\_\_\_HEALING POWER OF NATURAL FOODS  May Bethel . . . . . . . . . . . . . . . . . . . . . .  7.00
\_\_\_HERBS FOR HEALTH—HOW TO GROW & USE THEM  Louise Evans Doole . . . . . . .  7.00
\_\_\_HOME GARDEN COOKBOOK—DELICIOUS NATURAL FOOD RECIPES  Ken Kraft . . . .  3.00
\_\_\_MEATLESS MEAL GUIDE  Tomi Ryan & James H. Ryan, M.D. . . . . . . . . . . . . . . .  4.00
\_\_\_VEGETABLE GARDENING FOR BEGINNERS  Hugh Wilberg . . . . . . . . . . . . . . . . .  2.00
\_\_\_VEGETABLES FOR TODAY'S GARDENS  R. Milton Carleton . . . . . . . . . . . . . . . . .  2.00
\_\_\_VEGETARIAN COOKERY  Janet Walker . . . . . . . . . . . . . . . . . . . . . . . . . . . . . . .  10.00
\_\_\_VEGETARIAN COOKING MADE EASY & DELECTABLE  Veronica Vezza . . . . . . . . . .  3.00

## GAMBLING & POKER
\_\_\_HOW TO WIN AT POKER  Terence Reese & Anthony T. Watkins . . . . . . . . . . . . . . .  7.00
\_\_\_SCARNE ON DICE  John Scarne . . . . . . . . . . . . . . . . . . . . . . . . . . . . . . . . . . . .  15.00
\_\_\_WINNING AT CRAPS  Dr. Lloyd T. Commins . . . . . . . . . . . . . . . . . . . . . . . . . . . .  5.00
\_\_\_WINNING AT GIN  Chester Wander & Cy Rice . . . . . . . . . . . . . . . . . . . . . . . . . . .  3.00
\_\_\_WINNING AT POKER—AN EXPERT'S GUIDE  John Archer . . . . . . . . . . . . . . . . . . .  10.00
\_\_\_WINNING AT 21—AN EXPERT'S GUIDE  John Archer . . . . . . . . . . . . . . . . . . . . . .  10.00

## HEALTH
\_\_\_BEE POLLEN  Lynda Lyngheim & Jack Scagnetti . . . . . . . . . . . . . . . . . . . . . . . .  5.00
\_\_\_COPING WITH ALZHEIMER'S  Rose Oliver, Ph.D. & Francis Bock, Ph.D. . . . . . . . .  10.00
\_\_\_DR. LINDNER'S POINT SYSTEM FOOD PROGRAM  Peter G Lindner, M.D. . . . . . . . .  2.00
\_\_\_HELP YOURSELF TO BETTER SIGHT  Margaret Darst Corbett . . . . . . . . . . . . . . . .  7.00
\_\_\_HOW YOU CAN STOP SMOKING PERMANENTLY  Ernest Caldwell . . . . . . . . . . . . .  5.00
\_\_\_MIND OVER PLATTER  Peter G Lindner, M.D. . . . . . . . . . . . . . . . . . . . . . . . . . . .  5.00
\_\_\_NATURE'S WAY TO NUTRITION & VIBRANT HEALTH  Robert J. Scrutton . . . . . . . . .  3.00
\_\_\_NEW CARBOHYDRATE DIET COUNTER  Patti Lopez-Pereira . . . . . . . . . . . . . . . . .  2.00
\_\_\_REFLEXOLOGY  Dr. Maybelle Segal . . . . . . . . . . . . . . . . . . . . . . . . . . . . . . . . . .  5.00
\_\_\_REFLEXOLOGY FOR GOOD HEALTH  Anna Kaye & Don C. Matchan . . . . . . . . . . . .  7.00
\_\_\_30 DAYS TO BEAUTIFUL LEGS  Dr. Marc Selner . . . . . . . . . . . . . . . . . . . . . . . . .  3.00
\_\_\_WONDER WITHIN  Thomas S. Coyle, M.D. . . . . . . . . . . . . . . . . . . . . . . . . . . . . .  10.00
\_\_\_YOU CAN LEARN TO RELAX  Dr. Samuel Gutwirth . . . . . . . . . . . . . . . . . . . . . . .  5.00

## HOBBIES
\_\_\_BEACHCOMBING FOR BEGINNERS  Norman Hickin . . . . . . . . . . . . . . . . . . . . . . .  2.00
\_\_\_BLACKSTONE'S MODERN CARD TRICKS  Harry Blackstone . . . . . . . . . . . . . . . . .  7.00
\_\_\_BLACKSTONE'S SECRETS OF MAGIC  Harry Blackstone . . . . . . . . . . . . . . . . . . . .  7.00
\_\_\_COIN COLLECTING FOR BEGINNERS  Burton Hobson & Fred Reinfeld . . . . . . . . . .  7.00
\_\_\_ENTERTAINING WITH ESP  Tony 'Doc' Shiels . . . . . . . . . . . . . . . . . . . . . . . . . . . .  2.00
\_\_\_400 FASCINATING MAGIC TRICKS YOU CAN DO  Howard Thurston . . . . . . . . . . . .  7.00
\_\_\_HOW I TURN JUNK INTO FUN AND PROFIT  Sari . . . . . . . . . . . . . . . . . . . . . . . . .  3.00
\_\_\_HOW TO WRITE A HIT SONG AND SELL IT  Tommy Boyce . . . . . . . . . . . . . . . . . .  10.00
\_\_\_MAGIC FOR ALL AGES  Walter Gibson . . . . . . . . . . . . . . . . . . . . . . . . . . . . . . . .  7.00
\_\_\_STAMP COLLECTING FOR BEGINNERS  Burton Hobson . . . . . . . . . . . . . . . . . . . .  3.00

## HORSE PLAYER'S WINNING GUIDES
\_\_\_BETTING HORSES TO WIN  Les Conklin . . . . . . . . . . . . . . . . . . . . . . . . . . . . . . . .  7.00
\_\_\_ELIMINATE THE LOSERS  Bob McKnight . . . . . . . . . . . . . . . . . . . . . . . . . . . . . . .  5.00
\_\_\_HOW TO PICK WINNING HORSES  Bob McKnight . . . . . . . . . . . . . . . . . . . . . . . .  5.00
\_\_\_HOW TO WIN AT THE RACES  Sam (The Genius) Lewin . . . . . . . . . . . . . . . . . . . .  5.00
\_\_\_HOW YOU CAN BEAT THE RACES  Jack Kavanagh . . . . . . . . . . . . . . . . . . . . . . .  5.00

____ SEXUALLY FULFILLED MAN  Dr. Rachel Copelan  . . . . . . . . . . . . . . . . . . . . . . . . . . . . 5.00
____ STAYING IN LOVE  Dr. Norton F. Kristy  . . . . . . . . . . . . . . . . . . . . . . . . . . . . . . . . . 7.00

## MELVIN POWERS'S MAIL ORDER LIBRARY

____ HOW TO GET RICH IN MAIL ORDER  Melvin Powers  . . . . . . . . . . . . . . . . . . . . . 20.00
____ HOW TO SELF-PUBLISH YOUR BOOK  Melvin Powers . . . . . . . . . . . . . . . . . . . . 20.00
____ HOW TO WRITE A GOOD ADVERTISEMENT  Victor O. Schwab . . . . . . . . . . . . . . 20.00
____ MAIL ORDER MADE EASY  J. Frank Brumbaugh  . . . . . . . . . . . . . . . . . . . . . . . . 20.00
____ MAKING MONEY WITH CLASSIFIED ADS  Melvin Powers  . . . . . . . . . . . . . . . . . 20.00

## METAPHYSICS & OCCULT

____ CONCENTRATION—A GUIDE TO MENTAL MASTERY  Mouni Sadhu . . . . . . . . . . . . 7.00
____ EXTRA-TERRESTRIAL INTELLIGENCE—THE FIRST ENCOUNTER  . . . . . . . . . . . . 6.00
____ FORTUNE TELLING WITH CARDS  P. Foli . . . . . . . . . . . . . . . . . . . . . . . . . . . . . . 5.00
____ HOW TO INTERPRET DREAMS, OMENS & FORTUNE TELLING SIGNS  Gettings . . . . 5.00
____ HOW TO UNDERSTAND YOUR DREAMS  Geoffrey A. Dudley  . . . . . . . . . . . . . . . 7.00
____ MAGICIAN—HIS TRAINING AND WORK  W.E. Butler . . . . . . . . . . . . . . . . . . . . . 7.00
____ MEDITATION  Mouni Sadhu . . . . . . . . . . . . . . . . . . . . . . . . . . . . . . . . . . . . . . . 10.00
____ MODERN NUMEROLOGY  Morris C. Goodman . . . . . . . . . . . . . . . . . . . . . . . . . . 5.00
____ NUMEROLOGY—ITS FACTS AND SECRETS  Ariel Yvon Taylor . . . . . . . . . . . . . . 5.00
____ NUMEROLOGY MADE EASY  W. Mykian . . . . . . . . . . . . . . . . . . . . . . . . . . . . . . 5.00
____ PALMISTRY MADE EASY  Fred Gettings . . . . . . . . . . . . . . . . . . . . . . . . . . . . . . 7.00
____ PALMISTRY MADE PRACTICAL  Elizabeth Daniels Squire . . . . . . . . . . . . . . . . . . 7.00
____ PROPHECY IN OUR TIME  Martin Ebon . . . . . . . . . . . . . . . . . . . . . . . . . . . . . . 2.50
____ SUPERSTITION—ARE YOU SUPERSTITIOUS?  Eric Maple . . . . . . . . . . . . . . . . . 2.00
____ TAROT OF THE BOHEMIANS  Papus . . . . . . . . . . . . . . . . . . . . . . . . . . . . . . . . 10.00
____ WAYS TO SELF-REALIZATION  Mouni Sadhu  . . . . . . . . . . . . . . . . . . . . . . . . . . 7.00
____ WITCHCRAFT, MAGIC & OCCULTISM—A FASCINATING HISTORY  W.B. Crow . . . . 10.00
____ WITCHCRAFT—THE SIXTH SENSE  Justine Glass . . . . . . . . . . . . . . . . . . . . . . . 7.00

## RECOVERY

____ KNIGHT IN RUSTY ARMOR  Robert Fisher . . . . . . . . . . . . . . . . . . . . . . . . . . . . . 5.00
____ KNIGHT IN RUSTY ARMOR  (Hard cover edition)  Robert Fisher . . . . . . . . . . . . . 10.00
____ KNIGHTS WITHOUT ARMOR  (Hard cover edition)  Aaron R. Kipnis, Ph.D. . . . . . . . 10.00
____ PRINCESS WHO BELIEVED IN FAIRY TALES  Marcia Grad . . . . . . . . . . . . . . . . . 10.00

## SELF-HELP & INSPIRATIONAL

____ CHARISMA—HOW TO GET "THAT SPECIAL MAGIC"  Marcia Grad . . . . . . . . . . . . 10.00
____ DAILY POWER FOR JOYFUL LIVING  Dr. Donald Curtis . . . . . . . . . . . . . . . . . . . 7.00
____ DYNAMIC THINKING  Melvin Powers . . . . . . . . . . . . . . . . . . . . . . . . . . . . . . . . 5.00
____ GREATEST POWER IN THE UNIVERSE  U.S. Andersen . . . . . . . . . . . . . . . . . . . 10.00
____ GROW RICH WHILE YOU SLEEP  Ben Sweetland  . . . . . . . . . . . . . . . . . . . . . . 10.00
____ GROW RICH WITH YOUR MILLION DOLLAR MIND  Brian Adams . . . . . . . . . . . . . 7.00
____ GROWTH THROUGH REASON  Albert Ellis, Ph.D. . . . . . . . . . . . . . . . . . . . . . . . 10.00
____ GUIDE TO PERSONAL HAPPINESS  Albert Ellis, Ph.D. & Irving Becker, Ed.D. . . . . . 10.00
____ HANDWRITING ANALYSIS MADE EASY  John Marley . . . . . . . . . . . . . . . . . . . . 10.00
____ HANDWRITING TELLS  Nadya Olyanova . . . . . . . . . . . . . . . . . . . . . . . . . . . . . . 7.00
____ HOW TO ATTRACT GOOD LUCK  A.H.Z. Carr . . . . . . . . . . . . . . . . . . . . . . . . . . 7.00
____ HOW TO DEVELOP A WINNING PERSONALITY  Martin Panzer . . . . . . . . . . . . . 10.00
____ HOW TO DEVELOP AN EXCEPTIONAL MEMORY  Young & Gibson . . . . . . . . . . . 10.00
____ HOW TO LIVE WITH A NEUROTIC  Albert Ellis, Ph.D. . . . . . . . . . . . . . . . . . . . . 10.00
____ HOW TO OVERCOME YOUR FEARS  M.P. Leahy, M.D. . . . . . . . . . . . . . . . . . . . 3.00
____ HOW TO SUCCEED  Brian Adams . . . . . . . . . . . . . . . . . . . . . . . . . . . . . . . . . . 7.00
____ HUMAN PROBLEMS & HOW TO SOLVE THEM  Dr. Donald Curtis . . . . . . . . . . . . 5.00
____ I CAN  Ben Sweetland . . . . . . . . . . . . . . . . . . . . . . . . . . . . . . . . . . . . . . . . . . 10.00
____ I WILL  Ben Sweetland . . . . . . . . . . . . . . . . . . . . . . . . . . . . . . . . . . . . . . . . . . 10.00
____ KNIGHT IN RUSTY ARMOR  Robert Fisher . . . . . . . . . . . . . . . . . . . . . . . . . . . . . 5.00
____ KNIGHT IN RUSTY ARMOR  (Hard Cover)  Robert Fisher . . . . . . . . . . . . . . . . . . 10.00
____ LEFT-HANDED PEOPLE  Michael Barsley . . . . . . . . . . . . . . . . . . . . . . . . . . . . . 5.00

_____ MAGIC IN YOUR MIND  U.S. Andersen . . . . . . . . . . . . . . . . . . . . . . . . . . . . . . . . . . . . 10.00
_____ MAGIC OF THINKING SUCCESS  Dr. David J. Schwartz . . . . . . . . . . . . . . . . . . . . . 8.00
_____ MAGIC POWER OF YOUR MIND  Walter M. Germain . . . . . . . . . . . . . . . . . . . . . . . 10.00
_____ MENTAL POWER THROUGH SLEEP SUGGESTION  Melvin Powers . . . . . . . . . . . . . 3.00
_____ NEVER UNDERESTIMATE THE SELLING POWER OF A WOMAN  Dottie Walters . . . . . 7.00
_____ NEW GUIDE TO RATIONAL LIVING  Albert Ellis, Ph.D. & R. Harper, Ph.D. . . . . . . . . . 10.00
_____ PRINCESS WHO BELIEVED IN FAIRY TALES  Marcia Grad . . . . . . . . . . . . . . . . . . . 10.00
_____ PSYCHO-CYBERNETICS  Maxwell Maltz, M.D. . . . . . . . . . . . . . . . . . . . . . . . . . . . 10.00
_____ PSYCHOLOGY OF HANDWRITING  Nadya Olyanova . . . . . . . . . . . . . . . . . . . . . . . 7.00
_____ SALES CYBERNETICS  Brian Adams . . . . . . . . . . . . . . . . . . . . . . . . . . . . . . . . . 10.00
_____ SCIENCE OF MIND IN DAILY LIVING  Dr. Donald Curtis . . . . . . . . . . . . . . . . . . . . . 7.00
_____ SECRET OF SECRETS  U.S. Andersen . . . . . . . . . . . . . . . . . . . . . . . . . . . . . . . . 7.00
_____ SECRET POWER OF THE PYRAMIDS  U.S. Andersen . . . . . . . . . . . . . . . . . . . . . . 7.00
_____ SELF-THERAPY FOR THE STUTTERER  Malcolm Frazer . . . . . . . . . . . . . . . . . . . . 3.00
_____ SUCCESS CYBERNETICS  U.S. Andersen . . . . . . . . . . . . . . . . . . . . . . . . . . . . . 7.00
_____ 10 DAYS TO A GREAT NEW LIFE  William E. Edwards . . . . . . . . . . . . . . . . . . . . . 3.00
_____ THINK AND GROW RICH  Napoleon Hill . . . . . . . . . . . . . . . . . . . . . . . . . . . . . . 10.00
_____ THINK LIKE A WINNER  Walter Doyle Staples, Ph.D. . . . . . . . . . . . . . . . . . . . . . . 10.00
_____ THREE MAGIC WORDS  U.S. Andersen . . . . . . . . . . . . . . . . . . . . . . . . . . . . . . 10.00
_____ TREASURY OF COMFORT  Edited by Rabbi Sidney Greenberg . . . . . . . . . . . . . . . 10.00
_____ TREASURY OF THE ART OF LIVING  Sidney S. Greenberg . . . . . . . . . . . . . . . . . . 10.00
_____ WHAT YOUR HANDWRITING REVEALS  Albert E. Hughes . . . . . . . . . . . . . . . . . . 4.00
_____ WONDER WITHIN  Thomas F. Coyle, M.D. . . . . . . . . . . . . . . . . . . . . . . . . . . . . 10.00
_____ YOUR SUBCONSCIOUS POWER  Charles M. Simmons . . . . . . . . . . . . . . . . . . . . 7.00

### SPORTS
_____ BILLIARDS—POCKET • CAROM • THREE CUSHION  Clive Cottingham, Jr. . . . . . . . . 10.00
_____ COMPLETE GUIDE TO FISHING  Vlad Evanoff . . . . . . . . . . . . . . . . . . . . . . . . . . 2.00
_____ HOW TO IMPROVE YOUR RACQUETBALL  Lubarsky, Kaufman & Scagnetti . . . . . . . . 5.00
_____ HOW TO WIN AT POCKET BILLIARDS  Edward D. Knuchell . . . . . . . . . . . . . . . . . 10.00
_____ JOY OF WALKING  Jack Scagnetti . . . . . . . . . . . . . . . . . . . . . . . . . . . . . . . . . . 3.00
_____ LEARNING & TEACHING SOCCER SKILLS  Eric Worthington . . . . . . . . . . . . . . . . 3.00
_____ RACQUETBALL FOR WOMEN  Toni Hudson, Jack Scagnetti & Vince Rondone . . . . . . 3.00
_____ SECRET OF BOWLING STRIKES  Dawson Taylor . . . . . . . . . . . . . . . . . . . . . . . . 5.00
_____ SOCCER—THE GAME & HOW TO PLAY IT  Gary Rosenthal . . . . . . . . . . . . . . . . . 7.00
_____ STARTING SOCCER  Edward F Dolan, Jr. . . . . . . . . . . . . . . . . . . . . . . . . . . . . . 5.00

### TENNIS LOVER'S LIBRARY
_____ HOW TO BEAT BETTER TENNIS PLAYERS  Loring Fiske . . . . . . . . . . . . . . . . . . . 4.00
_____ PSYCH YOURSELF TO BETTER TENNIS  Dr. Walter A. Luszki . . . . . . . . . . . . . . . . 2.00
_____ TENNIS FOR BEGINNERS  Dr. H.A. Murray . . . . . . . . . . . . . . . . . . . . . . . . . . . 2.00
_____ TENNIS MADE EASY  Joel Brecheen . . . . . . . . . . . . . . . . . . . . . . . . . . . . . . . . 5.00
_____ WEEKEND TENNIS—HOW TO HAVE FUN & WIN AT THE SAME TIME  Bill Talbert . . . 3.00

### WILSHIRE PET LIBRARY
_____ DOG TRAINING MADE EASY & FUN  John W. Kellogg . . . . . . . . . . . . . . . . . . . . . 5.00
_____ HOW TO BRING UP YOUR PET DOG  Kurt Unkelbach . . . . . . . . . . . . . . . . . . . . . 2.00
_____ HOW TO RAISE & TRAIN YOUR PUPPY  Jeff Griffen . . . . . . . . . . . . . . . . . . . . . . 5.00


The books listed above can be obtained from your book dealer or directly from Melvin Powers. When ordering, please remit $2.00 postage for the first book and $1.00 for each additional book.

# Melvin Powers
12015 Sherman Road, No. Hollywood, California 91605